Finding the Path

Awaken Your Connection to Spirit

Kelvin Cruickshank

Copyright Page from the Original Book

PENGUIN BOOKS
Published by the Penguin Group
Penguin Group (NZ), 67 Apollo Drive, Rosedale,
North Shore 0632, New Zealand (a division of Pearson New Zealand Ltd)
Penguin Group (USA) Inc., 375 Hudson Street,
New York, New York 10014, USA
Penguin Group (Canada), 90 Eglinton Avenue East, Suite 700, Toronto,
Ontario, M4P 2Y3, Canada (a division of Pearson Penguin Canada Inc.)
Penguin Books Ltd, 80 Strand, London, WC2R 0RL, England
Penguin Ireland, 25 St Stephen's Green,
Dublin 2, Ireland (a division of Penguin Books Ltd)
Penguin Group (Australia), 250 Camberwell Road, Camberwell,
Victoria 3124, Australia (a division of Pearson Australia Group Pty Ltd)
Penguin Books India Pvt Ltd, 11, Community Centre,
Panchsheel Park, New Delhi – 110 017, India
Penguin Books (South Africa) (Pty) Ltd, 24 Sturdee Avenue,
Rosebank, Johannesburg 2196, South Africa

Penguin Books Ltd, Registered Offices: 80 Strand, London, WC2R 0RL, England

First published by Penguin Group (NZ), 2011
1 3 5 7 9 10 8 6 4 2

Copyright © Kelvin Cruickshank, 2011

The right of Margie Thomson to be identified as the author of this work in terms of
section 96 of the Copyright Act 1994 is hereby asserted.

Designed and typeset by Pindar NZ
Cover background images by iStockphoto.com
Prepress by Image Centre Ltd
Printed in Australia by McPherson's Printing Group

ISBN 9780143565352

A catalogue record for this book is available
from the National Library of New Zealand.

www.penguin.co.nz

Some names in this book have been changed to protect privacy.

TABLE OF CONTENTS

DEDICATION

In my life, I've had an amazing number of beautiful connections with spirit. At first I thought that it was normal and everyone could see what I was seeing, but I soon came to realise that was not the case.

It was the fantastic people in the heavens who showed me how to connect time and time again. They showed me how to listen in to their stories and hear about their remarkable journeys, becoming louder and clearer as I paid closer attention to them. I was so excited by this prospect of connection that I needed more. So I worked hard, setting down a good, solid foundation by meditating, visualising and talking to spirit every day. I found my faith in spirit grow as my trust in them soared. Without them, I could not possibly have found my own path to awaken my connection to spirit.

Knowledge shared is knowledge gained. I thank my spirit people and your spirit people for their love and guidance as always.

A special thanks to Margie Thomson, simply for understanding who I am and what I've been through, for her continued support and her wise words, which I will never forget.

To my kids, thank you for loving me unconditionally and for choosing me as your dad. I love you both with all of my heart.

To my true friends, who have always stood by me in my darkest hours, thank you for being with me in this life and undoubtedly in the next. Thanks for not giving up on me.

And to you, my readers, I thank you and wish you well in awakening your own connection to spirit. Enjoy the journey, work hard and remember to breathe.

Love always,

Kelvin and  spirit

STEP ONE

Opening to spirit

There are only two ways to live your life. One is as though nothing is a miracle. The other is as though everything is a miracle.

–Albert Einstein

I've been blessed with the gift of seeing and communicating with spirits since I was little. In fact, I can't remember a time when I couldn't see people who 'weren't there', or talk to 'imaginary' people. I just thought it was normal.

Sometimes it scared the living daylights out of me! I can remember as a little kid just curling up in a ball under my blankets at the end of the bed, trying to hide from the people I was seeing. Now that I've learned how to manage my gift, I love seeing spirits and working with them to help people. It's a daily miracle in my life.

Often that's why spirit will turn up when I'm around – they know that I can act as a go-between, bringing messages to their loved ones who are still living. But they don't always want something from me. Sometimes they just like to hang out with their living family and friends who might not even know they're there. But I do.

Not long ago I was out in my boat in the Bay of Islands, anchored out by the Cavalli Islands off Matauri Bay, which has to be one of the most beautiful places on the planet. Fishing is one of the things I most love to do in life. It's my idea of heaven, and if heaven involves a boat, a fishing rod and a beer or two, I can't wait to get there! But for now, Matauri Bay will do.

I was enjoying a quiet day, being part of the intense blueness of the sea, appreciating the dark green fingers of land that are part of the nature reserve there, and pulling the odd kingfish out of the water.

There was only one other boat bobbing around out there that day, a little tinny with a canvas hood – nothing flash. There were two guys on board, and all morning I watched them, the young guy holding his rod over the side, and what looked like his grandfather fussing round, cutting bait, fixing up the other rods. They seemed very companionable and I enjoyed keeping them in sight, as it reminded me of my own Poppa.

When I up-anchored and got ready to head back, I took one last look at where they were and sure enough their boat was still there. But now there was only one guy in it! The young guy was still sitting there with his rod – but where was the old guy? I called out as I went past, 'Hey, where'd your mate go?'

The young guy looked up, a little puzzled. 'Only me, mate! Just out here by myself today!'

You'd think I would have learned by now! This young guy had no idea he'd spent the day with his grandad in spirit, but I bet if I'd had the chance to talk to him about it he would have told me that he'd been thinking about the old guy, maybe remembering how they used to go fishing together. You see? We might not always know they're here, but they are, just keeping a loving eye on us.

Every day I'm reminded of this miracle – that through my gift I can link the ordinary, everyday physical world with the world of spirit, of white light and pure, eternal love. Spirit truly is the bridge from the impossible to the possible.

But the really incredible news is this: anyone can do it. Okay, I do believe that some people are especially gifted – just as some are especially gifted at being teachers, artists or builders. There are those of us who have always seen, heard, felt and smelt spirit, and for us the challenge has been to learn how to control this relationship so that it doesn't drive us crazy. Spirit can be very persistent and if you don't know how to handle it, you'll go nuts – believe me, I know all about that!

There are far more people who intuitively believe in spirit but struggle to get a sense of certainty in terms of their own personal experience. There are lots of reasons for this, and we'll explore some of them as we go along here. But my strong message in this book – and my reason for writing it – is that you don't need people like me to be the bridge between you and spirit. You can access spirit in your own life if you have the desire and the courage – oh, and the discipline. That last one, discipline, is really important, because without it, you won't make the progress you wish for.

We're all human; we all fall short of our own expectations at times. Let me tell you though: when you build a regular habit of sitting quietly by yourself, using some of the techniques that I'll show you to get in the meditative, spiritual zone, you'll find the experience so beautiful and satisfying that before long it won't seem like 'discipline', but more like something you simply won't want to miss.

Spirit is for everyone

Communicating with spirit in that quiet, meditative setting is one of the great joys of my life. It fills me up and makes me happy, it takes away any feelings of loneliness or aloneness that I might be experiencing, and it gives me the strength to go out into the world and do the things I need to do. To be in the presence of the Creator – which is what I believe I'm experiencing when I'm communicating with spirit – is to feel unconditional love. And isn't that one of the best feelings of all?

There's only one feeling that's possibly better than the feeling of being loved unconditionally, and that is to love. I love my kids – man, I'd do anything for them – and that's such a cool, powerful feeling. I love my work: through my contact with spirit, I'm able to help so many people, and that gives my life and my gift meaning.

Increasingly, I am sure it's through love that we touch the divine: that through love we can actually get close to spirit and begin to understand what the real truth about life is.

I have been so empowered in my life by my spiritual gift that now I want to share it. That's what my workshops are about and, to a lesser extent, my shows. They're designed to help people understand the process of spirit connection – as weird and wonderful as it is.

Of course, throughout history there have been people who have the ability to access the spirit world, to heal physical and mental illnesses, to prophesise, to bring forth messages from loved ones – and yes, sometimes to do harm as well. However, these people often held official positions within their community. In other words, they were treated as 'experts' or 'professionals' – the oracles of ancient Greece, the soothsayers of Rome, the stargazers of European courts, the sangomas of Southern Africa, Native American spirit guides and so on.

The revolution came in 1848 when sisters Maggie and Kate Fox communicated by making rapping noises with the spirit of a man who had been murdered and buried in their house near Newark in the United States. Word of this spread like wildfire, and modern spiritualism burst into life. Why? Because for the first time people realised that anybody could communicate with spirit – you didn't have to be in a priest-type role.

This was a breakthrough moment. In the resulting hysteria, even though there's not much doubt there were a few charlatans who were out to trick people in a kind of spiritual theatre – wherever people are at their most vulnerable, sadly there will be people there to take advantage – it was also the time for genuine mediums to come forward and inspire others.

So the message is: spirit is there for everyone. Having said that, however, I should also point out that not everyone's experience of spirit is the same. We all have different strengths, and spirit will manifest itself to you in a way that might differ from how it manifests to someone else. We can see, hear or feel spirit, and people often have a strength in one or more of these areas. We call these the 'clairs' – clairvoyance, clairaudience and clairsentience. Clairsentience – the ability to sense energies from other people and spirit, and which might just come as a whisper of breath across your face, for instance – is often the first to be activated.

Communication with spirit depends upon those qualities I mentioned before: courage and discipline in particular – and did I mention hard work? It also takes personal knowledge and self-confidence, so it's true to say that the path to spiritual connection is also a journey towards a better understanding of yourself. It can be no other way, for without that understanding of self, spirit can pull the wool over your eyes and lead you into places you might not want to go. Knowledge of self is an important tool for earthly life, too, right? It's all a really exciting journey.

It's only scary if you don't understand

As a small boy, and even into young adulthood, connecting with spirit could be scary for me. In those days it was always unsought. I didn't know what spirit wanted of me, and sometimes I assumed the worst because I was uneducated about how to deal with them.

Between the ages of about four and eight, I was terrified by a group of Maori warriors who came out of the bush and stood outside my bedroom window every night. We lived in a quiet, rural area that had seen much bloody, inter-tribal conflict a century and a half before, and I now know that these people were victims of that. But to a small boy, the sight of tattooed Maori warriors, in full traditional dress and weaponry, was nothing but terrifying, and of course I assumed they were threatening me in some way.

Then Pop, my grandfather, died and he too came to visit me, standing outside my window with the

Maori warriors. He told me they weren't threatening me, and explained that they were lost, unable to find their way to the next world. They recognised in me someone with the ability to communicate between the worlds, and that's why they were drawn to me, night after night.

Later, when I found my spiritual path and understood more, I returned to that house and faced the bush they came out of. I communicated with those souls and showed them how to find the light so they could at last cross over. This is classified as 'soul rescue' and involves love, prayer and, most of all, understanding.

In the years I've been devoted to spiritual work, I've met hundreds, perhaps thousands, of people whose lives have had a similar pattern to mine. That is, a childhood awareness of spirit, followed by a period of confusion and perhaps denial through adolescence and young adulthood, only to reach a point where the gift can't be denied any longer. The confusion and denial come through a lack of understanding, and also – and this can't be ignored – through the widespread denigration of the gift of communicating with spirit. So many of us have been told we are crazy – in fact, for many years I thought I was going mad, and simply didn't know how to handle my gift. I didn't even realise it was a gift!

Now, though, I sense a shift. Television has definitely helped. Programmes like *Sensing Murder,* and psychic mediums such as myself who have been televised around the world, have helped to spread a quiet message: that if you have the gift of seeing, hearing or otherwise sensing spirit, you are not alone. There are many other people just like you and, furthermore, your gift can be used to do so much good in the world.

But without that acceptance and understanding, people with the gift of spirit are doomed to experience fear and confusion as they struggle alone to make sense of the presences around them, and often misinterpret spirit's attempts at contact as an attack. If we had a more open and accepting society, children could more readily be told that, if a spirit wants your attention, you should treat it as politely as you would anyone else. You say hello, you ask what they want and you have a conversation. And, if your feeling is that this is not a positive spirit, you excuse yourself and tell them to go away. We will talk more about this later in the book.

As a small child, I was very isolated. Not only did we live right out in the wops, but my parents were very busy doing their jobs. So for me, spirit was incredibly significant. I'd be out the back, playing in the paddock or down in the gully behind our house, and people would appear to me and start talking. It was confusing and yet it felt kind of normal. I didn't realise that not everybody could speak to dead people.

What it did, though, was give me a feeling of being loved and connected – the opposite of what I often felt as a child in that lonely place. Nowadays, if I don't talk to spirit I feel terrible – lost, alone, sad, and as if no one cares. I know that's a funny way to feel, but it's an indication of the incredible love I feel coming from spirit. There's no doubt there are negative spirits, but the spirits I'm interested in come through on a connection of love – it's their love for us, and our love for them, that makes the connection possible. And the love of spirit is infinite, non-judgemental and very peaceful – who wouldn't want to experience that?

Nevertheless, there were times when I found spirit terrifying – when I felt they wanted something from me but I didn't know what, and they would become very persistent. Now, I think that those experiences were not meant to be negative – it was just that I didn't understand what they wanted.

School never suited me much – I was often bul-lied, and as I was dyslexic, I struggled to read. I was also the kind of kid who liked to be 'doing' all the time – off in the world, having adventures. 'I'm not here to eat my lunch' is one of my sayings! Sitting in a classroom never suited me, and I left school early to train as a chef.

In my first book, *Walking in Light,* I wrote about many of the experiences from my childhood that were brutal and emotionally challenging. They were tough times, but they were also my education for the work I do now. Every experience I've had, every feeling I've seen in the eyes of my assailants, every terrible thing I've seen happen to my friends – it's all filed away inside me and has become part of the menu by which I understand the messages I get from spirit.

I did push spirit away for a few years, but by the time I left school it was becoming more insistent, like a pounding at the door that just wouldn't stop. I thought I was going nuts.

Opening up at last

My first wife Rachael, who I married when I was 23, came from a Christian background. Together, we used to try out different churches around Hamilton, where we lived. We even tried the evangelist churches. One night she said she wanted to try a meditation course. I thought she was crackers – but really I was just scared about what would happen. I must have understood that meditation involved sitting quietly, and that was one thing I didn't usually allow myself to do, because of course that's when those freaky spirits came to see me. But she said we had to go, so we hopped on my motorbike and off we went.

There were quite a few people – living ones, that is – in the room and I was just leaning against a pole, actually feeling quite nice. Then a guy announced that he was going to light the candle and ask spirit to come forward. So they flicked the lights out and lit the candle. I realised that it was a bit too freaky, and I didn't want to be there. It scared me – when I closed my eyes there were all these things going on, and it was as if there was a party in my head. There was too much happening!

When it was over, I was very quiet. Rachael asked, 'How was that?'

'Oh, it was different,' I said.

'I didn't have much happen,' she said. She seemed a bit disappointed. 'I did everything he said, and I closed my eyes, but nothing happened.'

'Okay.' But inside I was thinking, 'What's going on?'

Then a friend suggested I get some Reiki healing. In those days I was a chef and working really long, hard hours. I think my friend thought Reiki would help my stress and exhaustion. I'd never heard of it before, and to be honest it seemed like a lot of mumbo jumbo. But it turned out to be a bit of a turning point.

Reiki is a Japanese technique for reducing stress that also promotes spiritual healing. Practitioners use their hands to connect you to life-force energy. If your life-force energy is low, you're more likely to get sick and feel stress. The word 'Reiki' actually comes from two Japanese words – 'rei', meaning God's wisdom or the higher power, and 'ki', which means life-force energy. So, put them together and what you've got is 'spiritually guided life-force energy'. It's pretty powerful stuff. I had no idea what I was letting myself in for and thought I was just going for a nice massage.

Reiki works to unblock our chakras – the spiritual energy centres on our body. A really important chakra is the sixth chakra, also known as the third eye, situated in the centre of our forehead, between our eyes. It is the third eye that we use for spiritual connection, and it is through this that we receive visions and all the cool stuff related to seeing, hearing, feeling and smelling spirit.

Many world religions associate this spot on the forehead with wisdom and spiritual insight. Hinduism and Buddhism believe it is the seat of enlightenment, and many Hindus wear a mark on their forehead to represent the third eye. Western philosophers have said that the third eye is situated in the pineal gland in the brain – the famous French philosopher René Descartes reckoned it was the seat of the human soul.

I knew nothing of all this, but when my Reiki healer placed her hands over my third eye, my head erupted in incredible pain, as if I'd been ripped open. Lots of symbols, images and snatches of languages came pouring into my consciousness. I didn't know it then, but she had opened my third eye, and from then on the images and visions I could see were so much clearer, and my sensitivity to spirit was increased even more. All I thought at the time, though, was that I had an incredible headache.

I've since learnt that this is not uncommon. There are exercises you can do to open your third eye – it is dormant or, at best, sluggish and sporadic in most people – and the exercises usually come with a warning that you might experience a headache or migraine for a few hours afterwards. With me, it was particularly intense because spirit wanted me fully open, fast, as they had plans for me, which you have seen.

Later I found out more about Reiki and there's a lot in it that I really like. Its healing is profound and is widely used in hospitals in the UK and the USA, before and after operations to reduce pain and fatigue and to improve recovery. In New Zealand, Reiki is offered to cancer sufferers through the Sweet Louise Foundation, a cancer support organisation, and through a small number of palliative care providers.

Its founder, Usui Mikao, came up with these guidelines, which are all about living a gracious life. I like them, because they're all about happiness, gratitude and kindness – three of the most important things in life, are they not?

Usui Mikao said:

> The secret art of inviting happiness
> The miraculous medicine of all diseases
> Just for today, do not anger
> Do not worry and be filled with gratitude
> Devote yourself to your work. Be kind to people.
> Every morning and evening, join your hands in
> prayer.

Not long after that initial experience, Rachael, our toddler son Javan and I went to live in Tonga for a while as I got a job chefing in a resort. Strange things happened to me there. For instance, this one time we were out walking and we went into a cave. There were all these dead people in there who looked like lepers. It turned out that the local villagers put all the sick people into the caves to die. I could see their spirits there as they'd not passed forward. But of course I still didn't know how to understand what I saw.

It was in Tonga that I opened my mouth and predicted our lives in the near future. 'When we leave here, we'll go live by the lakes and then I'll live by the ocean,' I told Rachael, and she said, 'You're just plain weird.' But that was exactly what happened. We left Tonga and we moved to Rotorua – the lakes. Then, after we broke up, I moved to Tauranga, right by the ocean. Go figure.

Things were becoming clearer, thanks to the Reiki healing I'd experienced, but I had yet to put in the effort that's required to truly access the enlightenment possible through one's third eye. That takes discipline and devotion – that is, conscious effort – and I didn't yet know enough about the spiritual zone to even know what was going to be possible. However, the Reiki healing did show me there were things happening for me that I seemingly couldn't stop.

Eventually I met some people who were able to explain what was going on. A woman I met recognised my gift, singled me out and gave me a reading. She told me she could see a friend of mine who had very recently passed. Her reading was so accurate, I was blown away. 'How do you do that?' I asked her. She looked me right in the eyes and said, 'All you have to do is ask, and they'll be there.' I realised suddenly how it worked, and that it was possible to harness this thing that had made me feel like a cork on the ocean for so long.

Unfortunately that woman turned out to be a negative influence, which I wrote about in *Walking in Light,* and she was interested in some very dark areas of spirituality. My spiritual involvement with her – which was very intense, as it was my first full-on spiritual quest – led to the breakdown of my first marriage, and to a personal mental breakdown as well. In hindsight, though, I was nevertheless on my way to a new part of my life where I took control of my gift and began to see how it could be used for good, not for personal power as that woman tried to do.

The next few years were really hard for me, as I've recounted in *Walking in Light.* I was homeless for quite a while, living out of my HiAce van. I lived on the streets and in the bush, eating possums to survive. And all that time I was finally consciously exploring the gift that I'd been born with – teaching myself to meditate, to pray, to ward off negative spirits and to bask in the love of my spirit guides and angels.

In those early years I found my own way forward, just by using my spiritual instinct. I used the Lord's Prayer for protection and meditated for hours, finally creating the quiet space around myself physically and also inside myself, so that spirit could come in peace and love and give me the messages I needed to hear.

For many years now I have worked as a medium, connecting people with the spirits of their loved ones who have passed. This is a blessing for me, as my gift is definitely all about helping people experience the peace and joy that comes through the white light of the spirit world. I know that I walk in the white light, which is the unconditional love of Jesus, God, the Creator, the Universe – whatever expression you prefer.

You can do this too

I love my work as a medium. I love to be connected with spirit, doing spirit work with people who are grieving over losing their loved ones, or hurting from past experiences. I am truly blessed. However, what I want people to realise is that you can do this too! Every one of us can find the peacefulness and pure love of spirit in our own lives. I'm not saying it's easy – it takes dedication, discipline and devotion – and it means stepping outside our daily business and distraction and actually making a time and a space for that spirit connection. But it's worth it.

In this book I want to show you how you can do this too, and of course I will share with you some incredible stories of how spirit has healed lives with love, tears and laughs.

We all have the answers to life inside us, just waiting to be discovered. It all depends on you –

whether you have the motivation to go and dig it out, and whether you're prepared for the truth from within.

On this journey, the most important thing you can have is an open mind. An open mind says 'yes' rather than 'no'. It considers all things. It opens doors, rather than closes them. An open mind is the key to creativity and growth and makes your potential truly limitless. Who knows how far you can go? Whether you think you'll fail or succeed, you'll be right.

Over the last few years, I've met many people like you: people on a journey to discover their spiritual potential. In this book, I'd like to share with you some of the stories I've been told. Spirituality is a kaleidoscope of different experiences, abilities and strengths. We can all take heart from these inspirational stories of how ordinary people have stepped out along the path of spiritual development. Sometimes they struggle, but sometimes they achieve real breakthroughs in their efforts to understand what life's all about, and to communicate with their loved ones in spirit.

ANDREW

Attending one of my day-long workshops was Andrew, a creative, spiritual soul. Despite having a lovely spiritual presence, and a strong desire to develop the sense of spirit that he'd had since childhood, he found that during one of the exercises he was unable to 'let go'. His high expectations of himself, coupled with his fear of failure, were blocking him from spiritual connection.

The exercise we were doing is one I usually do towards the end of the day. Everyone chooses a card from a pack of angel cards, and then, sitting in pairs, they 'read' their partner, letting the pictures on the card guide them into a deep understanding of the other person. Because we do this at the end of the workshop, most people are at the stage of feeling not only relaxed with each other but open to spirit. The flow is often incredible and the readings often very meaningful and accurate.

But Andrew found it difficult. He said that he just froze and couldn't seem to let go of his fears.

'I set a speed limit for myself,' he told us. 'I think perfectionism is a real problem for me.'

A lot of people will relate to Andrew's feelings, and for me the lesson is obvious: failure and the fear of it is only a feeling we generate within ourselves. It has a way of becoming real, but only when we breathe life into it. How do we overcome these feelings? You must have heard the expression, 'Feel the fear and do it anyway!' Like so many sayings, there is a bit of truth in this, but it's easier said than done.

Acknowledging – becoming conscious of your fear – is a crucial first step. You can't deal with any negative influence in your life unless you have named it and understood it.

Then, I believe, your success comes down to your attitude towards yourself. If you were talking to someone else about their fears and challenges, I'm sure you'd be kind and encouraging, wouldn't you? Why then is it so difficult to be kind, forgiving and encouraging towards ourselves, in our self-talk and self-thoughts?

Let's have another look at Andrew's story, because I believe there's a message here for us as well.

Andrew is an embracer of life. He left school at 15 to become a joiner. Apparently his teachers were disappointed as he was doing well at school, but he just had a powerful drive to get out into the world and start living. He's always been interested in the arts and has been a potter, a painter and a sculptor, as well as writing short stories. He finds that practising art creates a sense of peace in his soul.

Since early childhood, he's been aware of spirit. He had some scary experiences as a small child, feeling hands on his legs, and 'things coming out of wardrobes', but he also had some lovely experiences. He remembers asking his mother, 'Why do people have white light around them?' All his life he has seen people's auras, although not in colour – just a glow of white light. He tells me that when he attended my workshop, the room was glowing!

Then, when he was 11, he almost died from meningitis. He woke one morning in hospital and saw a monk sitting on the end of his bed, and he told Andrew he was going to be okay.

'It wasn't scary. It was very peaceful,' Andrew says. 'At that point I made up my mind that I wasn't going to die then.'

Nevertheless, in the intervening years he didn't focus on developing his relationship with spirit. He felt strongly that it was an area that really requires respect and that he didn't have the knowledge to experiment. I felt very humbled when he told me that it was when he saw the TV programme *Sensing Murder* that he gave himself the green light to get more involved with his spiritual side.

'It changed my life,' he says of watching the show. He saw there were other people unafraid of the spiritual connection, and also saw what a tremendous power for good it could be.

He gave up being a joiner and instead trained as a hypnotherapist. 'I actually see hypnosis as being very much the same as spiritual work,' he says. 'I'm helping people to go down to that place inside themselves where they're more open and more in tune so that their spirit guides can speak to them. If it's through me, or some words, or a metaphor, once we can get them into that alpha state or even delta then they're really open.

'I've always been interested in the way people think and how language can influence and persuade. Of course, I'm only interested in doing this in a just manner.'

In all this, he feels guided by his own spiritual guide or guides.

'I don't know anything about my guide,' he confesses, 'but I know there's someone at my shoulder telling me the right thing to say. I always ask for guidance with every client, and it's amazing that, in most cases, the rapport is built straight away.'

From all this I'm sure you can see, as I can, that Andrew is very spiritually blessed. He has chosen a career path that allows him to fulfil his spiritual side through helping others, and has intuitively developed a practice that works for him. He prays between clients, asking his spirit guide to let go the energies of the previous client, so as to be able to return to himself – something very important for those who work so closely with people whose needs can be great.

What I'm getting at is that when Andrew expresses his sense of failure, or his fear of failure, it pays to turn things around and look at the successes first, and then ask: where would you like to go from here? On this, Andrew is quite clear: his spiritual goal is to develop a more tangible understanding of his spirit guide.

He now knows there are particular steps he can take towards this goal and he has become disciplined in his approach. He prays every morning, and meditates later in the day.

'It took a while to be able to meditate properly because my mind races,' says Andrew. 'Now I have a place I go to, under a tree up on a hill. Once I've touched the bark, I know I'm there. I've found it really helps having a "tool". It's not unlike hypnosis.'

Since the workshop, he's taken my suggestion of going to the beach, drawing a circle around himself for protection and meditating. 'That's just fantastic. I feel absolutely safe.'

I believe that Andrew is doing everything right to develop his personal connection with spirit, and that it will lead inevitably to a greater sense of confidence and inner calm. When we ask for guidance, when we are regular and committed with our spiritual practice, we cannot fail to come closer to spirit. Cultivate your discipline, acknowledge your strengths, and allow your confidence to grow. And never forget to express gratitude for the many blessings already present in your life.

Meditation 101

Once you begin regularly practising meditation and prayer, you become stronger and more confident and more in touch with everything going on around you, including spirit. Meditation is the basis of my spiritual practice.

The first little baby step to take on the pathway to spiritual connection is simple: you just need to sit – or lie down – and be quiet. I know that sounds simple, but trust me, I know for some people it's not as easy as it seems. I'm someone who finds it very hard to sit still. The good news is that if you're like that, maybe meditation has even more to offer you than the average person. I can't stress enough how making time to do this basic activity actually feeds your life.

So: find a place. It doesn't matter where, as long as it's quiet and comfortable. It could be in your bedroom or lounge – the important thing is other people won't interrupt you. It could be outside sitting on your porch, or under a tree or in a hammock. You can sit on a chair, on the floor, or lie on your bed. You can even sit in the traditional lotus position, with your thumb and index finger touching – just make sure you are at ease, comfortable and alone.

Setting a good foundation is far more important than what position you're in. When things don't go right – when the wrong kind of spirits come to call, or when you can't make a connection – it's almost always because the correct steps have not been taken. It doesn't happen to me now but when I was just starting out, I had an embarrassing experience when I forgot to create the foundation for a reading: the spirits hung back and I was left high and dry. Served me right. I hadn't paid them due respect, or bothered to ask for what I wanted.

I believe in opening and closing all meditations with a prayer. This sets the scene really well, orienting us in the direction of spirit, and is a really important spiritual protection as well. So, take a minute to ask for guidance and protection as you begin this quiet, meditative time. I always use the White Light prayer below, but you might choose just to say something like, 'Spirit, protect me with your love. Show me how to get closer to you.'

White Light prayer

This is the prayer I say before every meditation and reading. It's very simple, but it works for me because I'm acknowledging and respecting my culture, my land, the angels, my whanau and my family that have gone over. And I'm asking Christ because I believe, as I always have done, ever since I was a kid, that he is the way and the truth and the light for me personally.

This prayer will leave you safe and focused. It is the foundation of my connection to spirit.

I ask to be clothed in a robe of white light, composed of love, power and the wisdom of God, not only for my own protection but so that those who see it and come into contact with it are drawn to God and healed.

I ask now for all negative energies and/or entities with me or near me now to be cleansed, raised and bound to the white light of the source.

I ask for the blessing of the angels of the white light to guide and protect. I ask for my tupuna, my ancestors, to look after me.

I ask for friends and family in the spirit world to show me what I need to learn today and help me to get closer to them, and for the spiritual awareness to strengthen our connection. I ask that we work together so that the healing of hearts can now take place.

I ask this in the name of the Father, the Son and the Holy Spirit, guardian angels of the white light, tupuna of our land. Kia ora, Amen.

Ready? The next bit is really nice. I want you to close your eyes and breathe! That's all. Now, feel where your breath is going. Many of us are in the habit of breathing very shallowly, so that the air comes into our chest and goes no further. I want you to visualise your lungs – they extend down a lot further than your chest. On your next breath, send that air right down to the bottom of your lungs. Don't strain – just let that air gently inflate your entire lung area. Breathe in with your nose and then release that air through your mouth. What are your shoulders doing? Sometimes they get tensed up, so be aware of letting your shoulders go as you breathe that air out of your body.

I want you to do this for five or ten minutes, depending on how you feel. Just focus on the in-out of the air in your body – make sure you're breathing nice and slow and comfortably.

What is your mind doing? If it's busy trying to spin all over the place, it really doesn't matter. When you become conscious that you're chattering away to yourself, just gently notice that fact and bring your attention back to the in-out of your breath.

This is all you're doing. You have no further expectation of this exercise than the in-out of the air, and a sense of ease and comfort in your body. Every now and then, bring your attention back to your shoulders and neck area. Are they relaxed? Good – carry on.

When you've had enough, bring yourself back to everyday life by opening your eyes slowly, and close the exercise with thanks. I usually say something like, 'Thank you for this experience. Please continue to guide me and bring me closer to spirit.' Take a further minute to reorientate your body before leaping to your feet and carrying on with your day!

This exercise is basic to meditation. It's the foundation of self-awareness, of quietening your mind and anchoring yourself in the now. It's how you make space in your life for spirit.

STEP TWO

Learning about the spirit connection

A mind at peace, a mind centered and not focused on harming others, is stronger than any physical force in the universe.

–Dr Wayne Dyer, self-help advocate and author

People often ask me where heaven is or, in other words, where the spirit world is. My answer is: it's right here, less than an arm's length away. It's not something you'll ever find with a telescope (not the usual kind of telescope, anyway!) as it exists on a different frequency to our earthly world and can only be reached when we change our own frequency through meditation and prayer. By changing frequency, I mean changing the way that energy actually hums through one's body.

It's not easy to pass between worlds. To talk with spirit, not only must I change my own frequency or vibration, but so must they. The way I conceptualise it is that we meet halfway between worlds – we step towards each other. What brings us together? Nothing but love – love is the motivation, love is the connection.

Every physical object has a vibration, an energy field – even that old chair you're sitting on right now! And we can, if we focus, be aware of the energy fields of the people around us.

EXERCISE

There's a simple, fun way you can get the feel of your own or a friend's energy field. Sit in a chair and have your friend stand in front of you. Close your eyes and focus as your friend brings their hand slowly down towards the top of your head. Say 'stop' when you can feel them – not their physical hand, but the warmth of their energy as it interacts with your own energy field, or aura. Reverse roles. Can you feel your friend's energy as you come closer to their body? This exercise is the foundation of spiritual healing: when I run my hands over a person's body, but without touching them, I can feel in my hands where their problems are.

Spirit is not, obviously, a physical object, but it certainly has an energy vibration, different and higher than our own. Through our spiritual practice, we aim to raise our personal vibration or frequency towards that of spirit.

Think of it like the dial on one of those big old radiograms. You have the dial set to your favourite radio station, but if you turn the dial slightly, first the reception becomes crackly and unclear, and then it shifts gradually into the zone of the next radio station – onto a different frequency. This is what we aim to achieve in our spiritual practice. But what we have to realise is that spirit, too, must change its frequency in order to meet us. This explains why it's hard for some spirits to come and visit – it's hard work and not easy to sustain the connection.

In my travels to different countries, I've come to realise that the miracle of spirit connection is underrated in New Zealand. New Zealanders say, 'Oh, okay, spirit connection, whatever. Why can't you get more details, rah, rah, rah.' We forget what an absolute miracle it is to get even a brief and simple message of love from someone who has passed. We're a practical bunch and we don't like to think too much beyond that piece of No. 8 wire that we can hold in our hands. In other countries, I've found that people are much more aware of the amazingness of this gift. I don't think we should belittle it. If spirit comes through for you, even briefly, that is an incredible effort on their part, and it is the most fantastic blessing.

You know how when you're drifting off to sleep, you eventually drift into that in-between state? You're neither asleep nor awake, but in that lovely fuzzy state. We call that the alpha state, where our brainwaves are in long, smooth wave patterns. Our body is relaxed; our minds are uncluttered, calm and receptive. It's a super creative space, great for learning – and perfect for connecting with spirit. How do we achieve it? By meditating.

We can also train ourselves to utilise that state while we are actually falling asleep – this is a great way of practising self-control and gaining control of our spiritual abilities. When I was a child I had an enormous amount of curiosity, and wondered whether I could hold myself in that fuzzy state so that I could 'see' what it was like to dream, and control my dreams and astral travel. I found I could. You know those dreams where you're falling off something, but you wake up with a big jolt just before you hit the bottom? I decided that I would stop myself from waking up, that I would take control of my dream. So that's what I did: I was falling, I yelled out 'Stop!' and I did stop falling, just before I hit the ground. Then I looked around me, and took off, flying – into my past, into my future, into other places altogether. This is a skill I used a lot during Sensing Murder *investigations, and explains how I was able to find where and how things had happened, and the details of a crime scene.*

However, if you're really committed to developing a spiritual practice that will lead you towards a strong connection to spirit, meditation is absolutely the key.

Line between the worlds

I believe that we all have at least one spirit guide who watches over us our whole life. This is most commonly a family member who has passed

– for instance, a grandparent – or it could be an unrelated guide who has been assigned.

When we seek to make connections to the spirit world from this earthly plane, I believe it is our spirit guide and the spirit of loved ones that we are most likely to meet. This is the safest kind of connection. These are spirits that we know have good intentions for us – who love us, in a word. We can more easily ascertain that they are who they say they are – and we'll talk more about that later.

But to my mind, the universe is like a gateau – you know, one of those cakes with several layers. We are here on earth, and the next layer is the spirit of loved ones who have passed, and then 'above' that, if you will, is the angelic realm and the Creator. There are many ways of visualising the relationship between our own world and the spiritual plane, but I find the gateau analogy is useful for people who are just starting out.

Another way to visualise our relationship with the spirit world is that we – our earthly existence, our physical world – are like specks of sand on the sea floor and that all around us and above us is the ocean-world of spirit.

To help people understand how spiritual connection works, I like to draw a picture which has us at the bottom. I represent us here and now with a circle, and then I draw a line connecting that circle to a star above us, which indicates heaven or, as I like to call it, 'home', and then another star above that which is the angelic realm. I draw an embracing heart around us and heaven. Inside this heart is the zone into which our loved ones in spirit can step to meet us, and into which we too can step once we've raised our frequency through our spiritual practice. It is a safe zone, created by prayer, and consisting of white light and love.

What does it feel like to step into this zone of white light? I liken it to when you step from outside into, say, a service station and you walk through what seems a curtain of air-conditioning – it's not dramatic, but it's a shift in temperature and air quality and your body registers that difference. Imagine you were blindfolded and you stepped from one room into another. Your senses would tell you that you'd changed rooms, wouldn't they? This is the subtle but unmistakable feeling of stepping from the physical plane to the spiritual zone.

When spirit come and stand beside you, it feels the same as if a person has just walked by you – you have that almost imperceptible impression of energy that is scarcely more than the feeling of a very light breeze on your cheek. We must be very alert, very observant, very focused to recognise them. It takes a lot of concentration to sustain contact with spirit, and can be very tiring for both spirit and for the medium.

The area outside the zone of white light is what we call limbo, where spirits who are not yet ready to move into the light reside. This is where the dark stuff hangs out – the lost souls, the ones who don't want to accept that they're dead and the ones who are demonic. This is where we often find people who have passed through suicide. They are sad and lost. These are people who have not learned to love themselves, and who are weighed down by bad feelings such as guilt, regret and perhaps anger.

This structural view of the spiritual realm is how it has been explained to me in my conversations with my spiritual guides. The spirits of loved ones may return to earth once they have healed and learned the lessons of their most recent earthly life – yes, I believe in reincarnation. I believe the angels are souls who have fulfilled their chosen journey, probably through many lifetimes. They are beings just like you or me but who have completed their journey, and now they have their wings. They can stay in the spirit realm – that is, they can come and go and visit us, but they are no longer tied to the everturning wheel of human existence.

You know, human belief systems are really interesting. I believe in reincarnation because that is what I have been shown by my spirit guides when I sit quietly in meditation. Can I prove it? No – but we'll all find out in our own time.

I've never been able to understand why the Christian church is so opposed to what I do – communicating with spirit – because is this not what Christ himself did, on a scale that is far beyond what I could ever hope to achieve? And is the Bible itself not filled with visionaries, prophets, people who could, in a nutshell, communicate with spirit?

I was brought up in the Christian church to believe that Jesus is the way, the light, the truth. I have never stopped believing that and, just as the Protestants believed that people could have their own individual relationship with God, without intermediary, so I have been gifted to have my own personal relationship with spirit. For me, my relationship with spirit confirms my belief in the Creator. Look how beautiful this world is! It's a masterpiece. I am privileged to connect with people from all walks of life, and I am often amazed at the beauty that is within people, too.

We all get stressed and drawn into business problems and life problems; we get busy and we forget about how beautiful this world can be. That's when meditation can bring us back and help us to appreciate the beauty that is all around us, and give us a sense of the full potential of our lives. We all need to be reminded of this. And in this moment of realisation, we connect with our God. I love that phrase 'God of our understanding'. God manifests in many ways – as white light, as Krishna, Allah, Buddha – but all these words are pathways to the same truth.

Make a special time

The incredible thing is that even if we don't realise it, when we think of our loved ones who have passed, they are there. The comfort this brings to the living is huge, and I've seen it probably thousands of times now. It never fails to move me, and to make me realise all over again the miracle of spiritual connection.

At one of my shows three sisters were sitting together, one of them holding a picture of a young woman.

'That's me!' whispered a woman in spirit. As I focused on her, I could tell that she was young – perhaps in her early twenties – and she went and stood behind the three. I was swept with a feeling of love and sadness, and I knew that the sisters were very much struggling with the death of their sister.

'She was the centre of our family,' one of the women told me. 'She was always so positive, she kept us all together. Our father is really broken over it.'

One of the women, the youngest, just sat there quietly with tears rolling down her cheeks, and I knew that her grief was almost too much, and she was in danger of ending her own life in despair. Her sister's death had left her with a feeling of the pointlessness of life, and she was in a black hole of depression.

In my mind I could hear notes from Bette Midler's song 'The Rose'. I asked about that, and the sisters all gasped. It was their sister's song – her name was Rose, and a friend had sung it at the funeral.

'Your sister was there, and she says the singing was unbelievably beautiful,' I told them. Then my head was filled with images of kauri trees, of all things.

'I'm seeing kauri,' I told them. 'Why would that be? They're making me feel peaceful and happy.'

They told me that not long before their sister died they'd shared a beautiful holiday in the kauri forests of Northland – their sister in spirit had chosen a lovely image to make them feel happy.

'Embrace the happy moments,' I told the three sisters. 'They are never forgotten. Your sister loves you and watches out for you and has nothing but happy memories of her time with you. But she wants you to go and live your lives now. It's okay to grieve and to be sorry and to experience those feelings of depression when we lose someone we love so much. We wouldn't be fully human if we didn't. But it's not okay to maintain that. At some stage we have to move on, to let those feelings go. This isn't the same as letting our love go. When we retain the tragedy – the negativity and drama of sadness and sorrow – it's not only us that can't move on. By being so sad, we tie them to us and they can't move on, either.

'Your sister is in spirit. She is beautiful and charismatic and full of love. I say "is", not "was", because she is still here and will always be here. You can't bring her back, but you can remember her and make time to say, "Miss you!" And when you do that, she'll be standing right beside you.'

The youngest sister wrote me an email the next day, and told me how much it had meant to her to get the message from her sister in spirit. 'I was in despair,' she wrote, 'and I've often felt like killing myself because I didn't want to have these feelings any more. But the message from Rose was so clear, I had no doubt that she was there, and that was so comforting. It made me feel that there is a point after all. It's still not going to be easy, but it's incredible to know that she's there with me, and that I can keep on loving her.'

I replied, and told her that when she needed to, she could make a special time to see her sister. She could find a quiet place where she wouldn't be interrupted, she could light a candle and put on 'The Rose', and focus on her breathing, and on thinking of her sister, and Rose would be right there with her.

The feel of a light breeze

If you want to become more spiritually developed, one of the important qualities you will need to develop is your observance. Pay attention: notice all the little sensations in your body and mind. Spirit contact is usually very subtle. Notice the feeling of a light breeze on your skin, goosebumps, or a ringing in your ears. If the ringing is in your left ear, it means a female spirit is coming through for you; if it's the right, it's male.

Spirit sends us plenty of little signs to let us know they're with us. Obviously, you wouldn't want to go overboard with this or you could start to go a bit loopy. I've met people who believe that everything is a sign from spirit, whereas it seems to me that quite often the things they are getting excited about are just nature doing its thing. A leaf falls from a tree. Is it a sign? No, it's a leaf falling from a tree because it's done its dash, it's had its life. That's the cycle of nature.

A sparrow flies past and people go, 'Oh my God, it's a sign, it's a spirit.' But is it not more likely that it's just a bird flying down to the café to get the crumbs from a plate?

However, if that sparrow flutters at your windows, and everything that's going on in your life at the time stops momentarily, I believe it is a sign or a symbol. It's like a frozen moment – there's just you and the sparrow, and the sparrow's staring at you, and then – chhhh – it takes off. That's a sign, because the sparrow, in our world, talks to us.

I know that sounds odd but the difference in synergy is very powerful. Sparrows carry a message of simplicity – their message is that our lives are too complicated, too stressful, and we need to chill and simplify. Other birds carry different significances. Fantails, for instance, are thought by Maori to be the spirits of those who have passed. But some people believe that if a fantail comes in your house, it means a death is imminent.

Mind your manners

Once I've made contact with spirit, I make friends with them. I'm polite and friendly, just as I would be with a living person. I say hello, ask how they're doing, and respectfully ask who they are and what they want. In a show, it's very important that I can bring forward from them the evidence that lets the living person in the audience know, beyond reasonable doubt, that this is indeed their loved one in spirit. We do this when spirit tells me things that I couldn't possibly know or guess.

Sceptics accuse mediums of 'cold reading', which amounts to educated guessing, based on body language. That's ridiculous. How could you ever guess the things spirit tells me? Unusual names ('Winifred' – I don't think anyone could cold read that!), important personal details ('the cookie bear club' – I hadn't even heard of it before spirit produced that as evidence for one client) or quirky little personal details ('apple cucumber' – who would be able to guess that the spirit had been an expert gardener, with a particular interest in apple cucumbers?). And so it goes. Collecting verifying evidence is such an important part of the process, and that is why I don't want living people in the audience bursting out with personal information – we must give spirit the time to come through with their own identification, so that we know they are who they say they are, and not a troublesome imposter.

Also, of course, it proves to everyone there that this is real. That's mind-blowing for most people, and opens all of us up to one of the great miracles of the universe.

Once we've established who's there, everything that comes out of my mouth is from them – I am truly the medium – the person in between the living and the spirit. It's not that I become them. They stand next to me and through pictures or feelings they give me the message they want passed on to their loved one.

This is not an easy form of communication. It's not as simple as sitting across a table from someone in a café, for instance, and just chatting. Sometimes it's hard to know what they are telling me. They'll say a name – repeatedly, passionately – but it seems to mean nothing to the living person. This is often because of expectations: the living have certain people in their mind that they expect messages from, but things don't work in such a straightforward way.

In one workshop, I was giving a quick reading to a woman when I mentioned the name 'Pat'. That was the name that the woman's mother in spirit was saying, quite emphatically.

The woman in the workshop told me that I'd actu-ally done a reading for her once before – more than a year previously – and her mother had brought the same message then, too.

'At the time I told you I didn't know any Pats,' she told me. 'But when I went home, it struck me that I had a cousin Pat who'd died – so obviously she's there in spirit with Mum.'

That was gobsmacking. I had no memory of that earlier reading as I do thousands, and I'm not fully conscious when I'm doing them, anyway. But here was the evidence that spirit was coming through: for the second time, a very specific, individualised message for this woman. How could I make that up?

Exactly the same thing happened during another reading. I was talking to a woman's mother in spirit, who apparently had been a very spiritual woman, as well as kind. 'She'd give you the shirt off her back,' I said. Then her mother began talking about Doris Stokes, the great UK medium who passed on in 1987, and she told me that she was now with Doris Stokes in spirit. 'You must have read Doris Stokes' book?' I asked the living woman.

'The last time I met you, you told me my mother was with Doris Stokes!' the woman told me.

Again, I had no memory of that, so is that not proof that spirit is real, when the messages are so consistent?

I often wish I didn't need to focus on this question of 'proof' so much, but that's human nature for you. Usually people need some form of personal experience before their doubts fly away.

Actually, on the subject of Doris Stokes, I have another amazing story to tell. In *Walking in Light,* I recounted how at the time I first became involved with the *Sensing Murder* television series, I had a strange and vivid dream about an elderly woman with white hair who insisted on a 'D' connection. I was chatting to one of the show's producers and told her about my dream. She was curious and sent me a photo, asking if it was the woman in my dream. And it was! It turned out to be Doris Stokes, whom I had never even heard of at the time. Since then I've always felt very connected to Doris, and she often pops up during readings to give me a hand.

But wait ... there's more! At the time of my dream, I was working on my very first case for *Sensing Murder,* that of George Engelbrecht, the 91-year-old who was beaten to death in his bedroom.

The *Sensing Murder* producer was so blown away by my dream about Doris that she did some research and found she had actually been in New Zealand around the time of that murder, way back in 1979, when I was only eight years old. What's more, she'd been interviewed on Radio New Zealand about the case. The producer subsequently found in the Radio New Zealand archives that Doris Stokes said she believed there were two assailants, one inside and one outside the house, and they didn't live too far away from George's house.

This was exactly the same conclusion that both Deb Webber (another psychic medium from the show) and I came to through our contact with George – a possibility the police began investigating after our programme aired.

Nothing beats personal experience

I was at a barbecue one evening when a man came up to me. He was a businessman, 60ish, conservative in his dress. He told me his name, and then he said, 'Well, I didn't believe in any of that stuff you do.'

'Oh, righto,' I answered, not sure where we were going with this conversation. 'No worries.'

'But boy,' he went on, 'you've changed our lives.'

He told me that his son had been shot, and he and his wife thought it was an accident until his wife came to me for a reading. I connected with her son, who passed on the message that he'd been murdered.

'We didn't believe you, but when it came to court, it did turn out to be murder. What you said to her and recorded with her came out in court, word for word, and they got him.'

This guy, this well-off businessman, had a big tear in his eye. And then he said to me, 'He's okay, isn't he?' And I said, 'Yeah, mate, he's good as gold.' I was really happy for him and his family as justice was served.

Put your own oxygen mask on first

One of the great challenges for us as human beings is how to love and help our fellow humans, while keeping ourselves intact in the face of problems that don't belong to us. This is always a particular challenge to me as it is the nature of my work that people bring me their most intense worries and sadnesses.

Doing readings for people who've passed violently, such as the young man who had been shot, or working on *Sensing Murder,* I really struggle with the things I'm shown. How do you deal with being shown horrific acts of violence against innocent people? I've seen little Alicia O'Reilly, six years old, being raped and murdered in her own bed; deaf Alexa Cullen being abused and killed; two-and-a-half-year-old Amber-Lee Cruickshank being murdered. That's very heavy stuff to deal with – and not only am I seeing it, but I'm actually experiencing the sensations.

In my daily work as a medium, I routinely deal with people experiencing extreme grief and loss and, every time, those feelings sweep right through me.

I don't want to stop having these feelings, because it's through experiencing the pain of others that I'm able to understand and help people – every experience I've ever come into contact with is stored away in my personal menu that allows me to interpret the messages of spirit. But neither do I want to live in a constant residue of other people's pain. And so I have had to learn to deal with it – just as people in other stressful jobs must: social workers, doctors, police and so on.

TANYA

A woman I met recently has an unusual job that's just as stressful as those I've already mentioned. Tanya works for a large bank, in a special unit set up to help people when their life circumstances change suddenly and they can no longer service their mortgages and other debts. So, in an average working day, Tanya gets calls from people who have been diagnosed with terminal cancer, or whose partners are dying, or who have been made redundant, or any one of a range of highly charged circumstances. These people are always very emotional, and quite often angry and aggressive.

'Some people revert back to childhood when they're in extreme circumstances, and they start chucking their toys out of the cot,' Tanya says. 'They get angry and they ask, "What are you going to do for me?"'

Within three months of starting the job, Tanya found that everything was breaking down: she was constantly getting sick and tired; emotionally she was a wreck. She was becoming emotionally attached to each and every customer, and found that sometimes their experiences resonated with things in her own past that she thought she'd dealt with but which suddenly seemed real again. She started to doubt decisions she'd made in her life, and to question how successful she'd been at moving on with her own personal issues.

Everyone else in her unit at work was much the same: stressed out, tense, unhappy – so Tanya worried about her workmates as well.

This was a dilemma, and it's one I can relate to. Tanya values the empathetic side of her nature, but she needed to learn how to be a caring person without killing herself in the process.

Tanya intuitively knew that the answer to her spiralling problems lay in developing the spiritual side of her nature. Actually, Tanya came up with a brilliant concept – a 'toolbox' of things that she's found helpful.

'I feel like I'm collecting lots of different things I use to help myself,' she explains. 'I have a fantastic counsellor who has helped me learn to meditate. I have great girlfriends and family who give me love and support. Then I went to one of your shows, and then a workshop, and that's given me something else really important for my toolbox – answers and direction.'

Tanya explained that for a very long time she had been communicating with spirit, but hadn't known what was going on. She told herself it was just talking to herself. However, in one of the shows, for the first time she gained clarity and realisation where that other voice was coming from, and how it related to her own voice.

'Also,' says Tanya, 'to be honest, being in the workshop setting made my experience acceptable and normal, not scary and crazy and unusual. For the first time I can be open about it, and that gives me courage and empowerment to go further and further.'

Tanya's grandmother died when she was a child – 35 years ago. Ever since, Tanya has had a constant sense of her grandmother in spirit. 'I didn't realise it was her ... well, I sort of did, but I wasn't sure.' What she knew was that there was an almost constant 'other' presence with her, talking to her, showing her images. 'Sometimes the noise just got too loud. I told my mother about it, and she said, "Just tell it to bugger off." I did, but that made it worse. I know now that the way to deal with it is to take some control, to tell them that you love them, but not now because I'm tired.'

Tanya is now filled with the exciting realisation that the stress and illness of the past year had a purpose. 'I think I was on a journey, that I was heading to this point anyway. That I was meant to be sick for the last year so that I could learn to let go of the last 40 years and start on the next 50. So for me, going forward, the question is: where to from here?'

Taking control and placing boundaries around her own energy have proven to be the key answers to the problems in Tanya's life. It has helped her understand and get control of her grandmother in spirit; and it has helped her come to terms with her day job.

She now knows not to engage so closely with her customers. She sticks as best she can to the guidelines to offer them practical help – trying to keep the conversation professional and the client engaged, but remaining emotionally detached. This sounds simple, even obvious, but to someone like Tanya who is used to engaging in snowballing emotional encounters where her empathy was never, ever enough, it's immensely empowering.

The answer for Tanya has lain in meditation, which she says strengthens her ability to clear her mind so that it's not 'so cluttered, so full. I've never been able to do that – it's always been full, and full on. Meditation has given me the ability to communicate with spirit in a structure, a give-and-take exchange, and be able to turn it on and off when I need to. Hopefully by doing this consistently, my physical presence won't be so tired as it has been this past year.'

Now, after every customer phone call Tanya mentally visualises leaving all the troubles with the person they belong to – actually removing their troubles from herself.

'I initially took this job because I wanted to help people. It's as simple as that. And it's been a steep learning curve, but now I've started to take the lead over how I want to help, not just helping for the sake of it.

'I've been learning about putting on my own oxygen mask first before I can help others. I was running out of energy and didn't know how to re-fuel. Now I've learned that I don't need to go three months before getting sick in order to refuel. I can do it every day through meditation and positive communication with spirit, and then I won't ever run low. If you are a martyr and a saviour you will put everyone first. I've done that my entire life but now I know that's not really the best way to help people. I used to think that my energy was limited and I could only do so much. But now I know it's boundless and limitless. I can find the strength and the support to do more and help more.

'You never stop learning, you never stop grow-ing. It's good, it's very good.

'We all need to walk our own path. We all need to create our own little toolbox – filled with things that are going to help you. Technology has made us lazy. We live in a world where everything comes with instructional DVDs, DIY and How-To manuals. There's no instruction manual for life. Just as there is no instructional DVD to finding your own path to spirit. We need to work diligently, secure in our own faith and move forward in our own unique way.'

My modus operandi

As Tanya has discovered, meditation coupled with prayer are the keys to spirituality.

When we set out to meditate, it is vital to create a good foundation. Even though I've been meditating for many years, I am still very careful about it every time I meditate as it's an integral part of the experience – I can't stress this enough.

First, I make sure that the space I'm going to be meditating in is comfortable and quiet, and that I'm not going to be interrupted. Very importantly, I turn off my cell phone! I like to put on some nice, spiritual music, and I light a candle. Some nights I just sit with a candle in front of me and I don't say anything to myself. I just breathe through it. You'll be blown away by some of the things that come to you, just by being quiet.

Having a candle flickering is a very, very good thing. It both emits light and draws light in. It's a symbol of the light we have within ourselves, and also of the white light of spirit. We can all recognise the symbolism of candles. When people get killed in plane crashes, everyone holds a candle and a vigil. Churches have candles. It's symbolic of the spirit: when the light is shining, it says 'draw near'.

But the other thing about a candle is that it flickers, and that helps you go into that flickering eye motion that activates your third eye and helps you get into the zone.

The main thing is that a lit candle helps your mind relax. It brings serenity and can reflect the spirit presence in the room. It will burn completely straight. There might not be a breath of wind in the room, but when you say your prayer – 'I ask to be clothed in a robe of white light' – it will flicker all of a sudden as you enter your meditation.

I say a prayer to protect my environment, asking for the white light to be over my room for the length of time that I'm going to be meditating for. I believe that prayer is very individual – it expresses the heart of the person praying, and there is no right or wrong in the words you choose, other than that they are truly meant. There are really only two prayers that I use – the Lord's Prayer, and the prayer asking for the protection of the white light. I love the white light prayer, so I just change it a bit depending on the situation I'm in.

Finally, I ask for spirit to guide me to understand the things I need to understand.

But I can't concentrate!

Yes, it's sometimes hard to focus. This is where discipline and practice come in. Don't expect amazing things to happen all at once. It's a step-by-step process as you work to gain control over your mind, and begin to access your true self.

We all live ridiculously busy lives, and our minds fizz with so many issues all the time: our jobs, our family relationships, arguments with friends, money

... These thoughts will sense the space you're creating and try to rush in and claim it.

Don't try to push them away. Remember how Tanya's mother told her to tell her grandmother in spirit to bugger off? It didn't work, did it? The way to lessen the noise of troublesome spirits or troublesome thoughts is perhaps counter-intuitive: accept them. Acknowledge them, and then politely put them to one side. I will say to spirit, 'Hello, I acknowledge you, but I can't talk to you right now.' With thoughts, it's much the same. I allow myself to go through those thoughts and feelings, and I sort them and box them.

I ask myself, 'Can I sort this out here and now?' Well no, but I know it's there and when I come back from my nice meditation I'll be able to deal with it better because I'll be a lot calmer. So, I put it to the side. And as I work through those issues I am able to become more peaceful and get into that other zone.

Now, here's the thing. Most people in this Western world believe they can push everything to one side and just meditate. And although they try really hard, nothing happens! Why? Because instead of respectfully acknowledging the things in their mind, they struggle to push it all out, and it comes back and bites them on the backside.

As we move through this book we're going to do some lovely meditations, but they all come back to the basics – if you've set yourself a good foundation you'll be fine, and you won't need to have any fear.

Meditation

GETTING GROUNDED

I ask for the protection and love of the white light. I ask for a peaceful mind, I ask for patience so that I can set aside my expectations and understand the lessons that spirit has for me, and I ask for the strength to pursue my goal of spiritual awareness.

Our lives are so busy and distracting that the effect on our minds is like a great scattering – our thoughts and our energies are scattered all over the place. We say we're 'in the clouds' and we mean that we can't find a good footing for ourselves. In a word, we feel ungrounded.

Being grounded is about pulling all those scattered thoughts and energies back into your body, standing strong and firm and balanced within yourself. I find that visualisation is really helpful here: if we send our thoughts in a particular direction, our feelings will follow.

With this exercise, the most important thing is that you feel comfortable – both physically and psychologically. But it is particularly good if you can stand outside. If you have to be inside, and if you need to sit or lie down, that is still fine. But I'll talk you through as if you're standing outside.

Take off your shoes so that you can stand barefoot on the ground. Place your feet a shoulder's width apart, so that you're very stable.

Close your eyes and begin your breathing, as we did in the first meditation exercise. Breathe in through your nose, and out through your mouth, remembering to check in with your shoulders and neck to ensure they're not tense but are releasing as you release the air from your lungs.

When you've brought yourself into focus with your breathing, begin to notice the way your feet feel upon the ground. Feel the earth, and feel your connectedness to it. This is a very physical sensation: your firm feet, the cool earth.

Now, imagine that you are not only standing firm upon the earth, but are sending down roots below the surface, into the earth itself. You are literally earthing yourself. Visualise a tree – many people choose an oak, but I always visualise a kauri tree: straight, strong, and able to withstand any storm. Think of yourself as that tree. Feel what it's like to stand so tall and strong. Feel your body lengthening, stretching upwards in your mind, as your feet become even more rooted in the earth.

Allow yourself to feel the strength of this earth connection. Bring your focus back to your breathing – in and out, in and out. You are truly at one with the planet.

When you feel you want to end this meditation, refocus on your breathing, and open your eyes slowly. Remind yourself of the feel of your feet, so solid on the ground. Acknowledge the way your body is feeling – strong and at one with itself. When you're ready, thank spirit for giving you this experience, and return to your day.

When I do this exercise, I feel my stress melting away. I feel calm and reintegrated with myself. I also feel very aware of my bodily sensations, and this is so important to cultivate. It is the skill that will help you identify when spirit – the 'other' – joins you in the zone.

STEP THREE

Know yourself

Inner growth is a slow and incremental process that accomplishes extraordinary results through what often look like minute daily changes.

–Ingrid Bacci, healer, author and inspirational tutor

Who are you? Why are you here? Are these not the big questions of our earthly life? When we come close to spirit, we approach answers to these questions. Spirit fills us with love and the knowledge of love, and that knowledge brings us a great feeling of purpose.

When I communicate with spirit, I feel whole – my own soul feels full, happy and right. I tune in to all the good things of life: peacefulness, joy, love. It is an expanded feeling. I begin to feel at one with the world.

This is how it should be. I believe that just as it is our earthly goal to heal ourselves as human beings and to make our souls whole, equally, when we do that we begin to sense that we are simply a part of one giant spiritual whole. So when we heal ourselves, we also help to heal the world.

When we communicate with spirit we experience the interconnectedness of all things, and, at a very basic level, our perception of life is blown apart. Perhaps we feel purposeless in our own existence, or limited, fearful or alone. Perhaps we are overwhelmed with negative thought patterns that hold us down like a heavy weight. But when we reach out to spirit, things must change. How can we be purposeless when we realise that we are part of an incredible whole; how can we be fearful or limited when spirit tells us that nothing is impossible; how can we remain trapped in our sludge of negativity when our experience of spirit is of purity and absolute love?

Throughout human history, people have asked these big questions and pondered how to see themselves in relation to the universe. To me it's quite simple – miraculous and mystical, sure, but simple nonetheless. Through our own experience of meditation, of creating that opportunity to let spirit flow through us, we understand at the level of our own consciousness and perception that all is one; we ourselves are part of a loving whole that incorporates all of life.

There are different ways of knowing, and in Western culture in particular we've become obsessed with left-brain knowing. That is, we know that our brains are made up of two halves – the left side and the right side. Put simply, the left side is more concerned with empirical knowledge – facts and logic – while the right is to do with creativity and intuition. Our society emphasises the importance of knowing something in a logical sense – can it be problem-solved and understood scientifically?

However, as many cultures throughout world history have allowed, there is another way of knowing, and that is through our hearts, our feelings and our experience – through the right side of the brain.

And, just as an aside, who knows what science will come up with in the future? It's the nature of science to keep pushing forward in its understanding. There is already new research linking quantum physics to a different understanding of the universe, space and time, and to a new understanding of human consciousness. Some scientists are already saying that their new understanding of the zero-point field points to the possibility of a universal energy source, maybe even including spiritual survival after the death of the body. Pretty amazing, huh?

But the fantastic thing is, we don't need to wait around for science to prove what we already know – in the very deepest sense – for ourselves. This is the most beautiful message of all: spirit is there and able to be experienced, personally, by every single person.

Now is where you'll find spirit

If you take a look at the way animals behave, it can teach you something about the way humans live their lives. If you observe any of the animals likely to be around you – dogs, cats, sheep, whatever! – you'll notice that they are fully involved in whatever they are doing, right now. They are utterly, fully engaged in the business of 'now'.

Take a look at the humans around you – in fact, take a look at yourself. Where do you spend most of your mental time? Most of us spend an awful lot of time in the past – and that usually involves wallowing in feelings of guilt, regret, sadness, resentment – or in the future, where you'll find fear, trepidation, anxiety and self-doubt.

These feelings are emotional and spiritual traps. They are like weights on our feet and, worse, weights on our souls. They are all about the fact that we live in the past and the future but scarcely ever stop to just experience now. And let me tell you something really important: it is *now* that you will meet spirit. It's not in the past or in the future, but when you actually quiet down, sit in prayer or meditation and anchor yourself in the most positive way to the present. That is the only place you will encounter spirit.

However, the worst thing is, most of us are so out of touch with our inner beings that we're not even fully conscious of the thoughts and feelings that prevent us from moving forward into a more satisfying spiritual life.

Here's my point: if we're not fully conscious beings, aware of our own feelings and thoughts, we will not be able to progress spiritually.

Did you know that there is a close relationship between thoughts and feelings? Go on, try this exercise to see what I mean.

EXERCISE

Put a thought into your mind that reflects one of your core attitudes to yourself. Maybe it's something like: 'I'm a terrible mother/father/friend/partner', or 'People are always out to get me' or 'I only attract negative people into my life'. Maybe it's even, 'I'm useless at meditating'.

Now, listen to your body. How did it respond to that thought? Feel down into your stomach, your chest, your legs, your fingers – did they have a reaction to that thought? What happened to your heart when you said that to yourself? I bet there was a reaction on the physical level to that thought you put into your mind. It's impossible to hear such harsh and negative messages about ourselves and not also feel very heavy emotionally and physically.

The feelings that come in response to thoughts of guilt, resentment and fear are what we call very low-frequency feelings – they contain low, negative energies. To communicate with spirit, we need to raise our frequency. Spirit operates at a very high frequency, and the higher we can raise our own vibration, the closer we come to spirit. It is in the high vibration state that we can experience and communicate with spirit. But to get there, we need to do something about the negative feelings. In other words, we need to deal to all the bad mental habits we've got ourselves into.

I sometimes think that learning to communicate with spirit is another form of self-help. Spiritual counselling? Why not!

In my workshops, the first thing I get people to do is to write down on a piece of paper how they feel at that moment. Now I'd like you to do some work, too.

I suggest that you find a notebook for this section. It will be very useful for you to be able to look back at where you began. It's always really positive to be able to say to yourself, 'That was how I felt then; this is how I've changed.'

Even if you think you are very emotionally confused, you'll be amazed at how regularly focusing on your inner self will help you achieve some clarity. It's like switching on a torch. All the information is waiting there inside you, if you just switch on the torch of your consciousness and actually go looking for it. But please: it doesn't all happen at once. Try and set aside your expectations: they're a killer in both the earthly and spiritual realms. Just go with the flow and be patient.

EXERCISE

Okay, so first, let's have a look at where you're at in your life. Take your time over this. Think deeply: what are the important, defining characteristics of your life, and how do you feel about them? We are not interested in assigning blame or making excuses. That can never help you. Blame and excuses are like sticky fly-paper: they trap you and stop you from moving forward.

For instance, if you're having relationship problems, simply say, 'I'm arguing with my partner a lot at present' or 'I feel distant from my partner at present' – rather than writing about what a terrible person your partner is.

Right, here are some questions to focus your thinking:

- *Do you have a job that you are satisfied with? Are you on a career path that fills you with energy and hopefulness?*
- *Are you happy with your relationships with your children/your parents?*
- *How do you manage your finances? Do you have a lot of debt?*
- *Do you live in a home that reflects you in a positive way?*
- *Are you connected to your community?*
- *Do you make time for yourself every day? Are you satisfied with this?*

- *Do you have a regular spiritual practice? Are you happy with this?*
- *What are the other things that are important in your life?*

This list will eventually be a combination of objective facts and significant feelings about your life as it actually is right now.

Tip: Don't just write single words like 'happy' or 'sad'. Really explore those feelings. How does it make your body feel? Try and become more descriptive, as this will help you better understand the feelings that you experience. For instance, if you say that you are happy with your relationship, describe that sensation of 'happiness': perhaps you feel secure, valued, entertained, listened to. If you say that you're not happy with your financial situation, is that because you spend too much, and try to fill yourself up emotionally by buying things, for instance? Or do you have too much debt and therefore feel frightened and insecure? Really try to name your feelings.

EXERCISE

Now, let's look at your dreams and aspirations. This might seem like a weird thing to think about, but what would you like to have said about you at the end of your life here on earth? Pretend you are writing your own obituary – the one that, if all your dreams came to fruition, you would like to hear read out at your passing. This will cover your relationships, your personal ambitions, your role in your community, your sense of adventure, your sense of style, your creative achievements – everything you can think of that you would like to achieve in your wildest dreams.

Tip: this isn't as easy as it sounds! Your left brain 'logic' – which is often just a learned negativity towards yourself – may try to sabotage you. Be firm with yourself. Tell yourself, 'I hear this negative voice, but I will choose to set it aside while I do this exercise.' Let your right-brain dreamer really come into play in this exercise.

EXERCISE

Now go back to your first list. On a fresh page, draw a line down the middle, lengthwise. Looking at your objective assessment of your life – the facts and feelings that make up your daily life – what are the things you would like to change or even get rid of, and what are the things that you would like to keep?

Tip: For some reason, it's often easier to pinpoint our dissatisfactions rather than the positive things in our lives – perhaps this is because of perfectionism. We might be very happy with our partner, yet aware that things aren't perfect. Indeed, there is always room for improvement in all human relationships. But be careful about this: does this mean we want to get rid of our partner? Perhaps we can cultivate a more joyful and accepting attitude – to enjoy what is, rather than what we think it should be.

Don't be afraid to acknowledge that there are things in your life that you are happy with and want to keep!

Let go – in a positive way

I know there are relationships that are damaging, abusive and even violent, and if you are in one of those, you need to very carefully consider why you are in a relationship of that sort. It is not enough to blame your partner; that attitude will only entrench you further in what is a very negative and possibly dangerous experience for you both. Such a blaming attitude will not help you on your spiritual journey. Ask yourself instead: what is your role in the relationship? You are in that situation, are you not? Something about you and your feelings about yourself have led to you choosing to be right where you are now. While you can talk to your partner about how you see his or her behaviour, you can't actually change them. Only they can do that. And only you have the power to change yourself and your own situation. By asking yourself what your role is, you are taking a step out of the glue-like stickiness of your blame, resentment and fear, towards accepting a more powerful role in your own life. As you make those changes in your own life, the negative relationships will either change too, or fall away because you will no longer have use for them.

Often when people are in a negative and damaging relationship, their friends will tell them to 'let go' of the relationship. But without self-knowledge, it's not that simple. They might let that man/woman go but, without becoming clear about their internal motivations – weeding their own garden, if you like – they will just walk into an identical relationship. The same point is true for any situation that you go on repeating even though you don't really like it.

Some people just jump from ship to ship. What I think is that, yes, it's important to let go, but truly letting go means acknowledging the way you feel in this situation, becoming fully conscious of what you were going through, what the signs were – and then making a decision for yourself that you no longer accept that type of personality in your life. You set yourself free, and you set them free as well.

It's the same with a death. Sometimes people try to hold on after someone has passed, wishing they were still here, becoming very depressed and obsessed. They actually become a victim – a spiritual victim. They are angry and blaming and cannot let go of either their loved one, or their negative feelings. They cling on to their desire to control the uncontrollable. I think that if they looked further into themselves they would see that their difficulty lies somewhere within themselves, and not with simply missing the person who has passed.

To be spiritual is to really examine yourself, I think. Truly look at yourself. You won't be able to let go until you do.

On earth as it is in heaven

The way we conduct our earthly relationships and engage with the people we love is a big part of our spirituality. Through our relationships we experience and learn about love, and through our earthly loves we can become more aware of the possibility of the eternal love of the spirit.

Sometimes we are held back from spiritual development because we have unresolved feelings about our earthly relationships. For instance, perhaps we grew up in a family that didn't display affection, and so we have struggled to learn how to be open and loving in our own adult relationships. Many of the messages I get from spirit concern this. When people pass, they have the opportunity to review their life on earth, and sometimes they want to let their living loved ones know that they are now sorry for the way they conducted their earthly relationships. This can be hugely meaningful to the living, and can give them the ability to move on in life with renewed confidence, knowing they are loved.

During one of my shows a man in spirit came through, wanting to talk to his daughter. It turned out that this man was a bit of a hard guy when he was alive – not a bad guy, but certainly not someone who showed much softness to his family. He was impatient and his family had learnt to keep their distance for fear of annoying him. Nevertheless, there was still a lot of love and loyalty – it was just that things could have been better if he'd been more openly loving.

During my show, however, the man came through transformed. He told his daughter he was 'as free as a bird now' and really regretted that he hadn't been more emotionally relaxed during his time on earth. His daughter was very moved by his message – it was just what she needed to hear, as she'd always loved him and wanted to be closer to him.

The father showed me an image of a pair of spectacles. I wasn't sure what he meant, so I told the daughter. She laughed, and told me, 'I wear his glasses now!' That was such a clear message that her father could see her and was with her.

Then things got serious. I received an image of a racing motorbike, a racetrack, and a sensation of extreme danger. The daughter agreed that her sons both raced motorbikes.

'Please! Be safe!' was the urgent message from her father in spirit. I hope she was able to communicate that message to her sons. Sometimes these messages from spirit can save lives. But for this woman, the feeling of softness and love that she received from her father was also life-changing. Messages like that can free someone up, and give them the confidence to live their own lives more happily and with greater emotional openness.

This story is not as dramatic as some readings I do, but I particularly like it because it shows us something very important about the afterlife: that all the judgement we experience on this earthly plane falls away. In the afterlife, there is no judgement. It disperses, and souls – even of people who did not like each other on earth – can reconnect. Souls are at peace, and through people like me, they can also make peace with their loved ones left behind. Such is the blessing of messages from our loved ones in spirit.

As you develop your own personal spiritual practice, you will also come to know this confidence that comes from experiencing the non-judgemental love of spirit. By the way, I love the term spiritual practice – because we do have to practise in order to advance.

The power of thought

Now, back to your list of things you want to do and be.

Do you know that you have complete power over your life? Do you know that you create your own reality? The key is: do you know what it is that you really want?

When you make a list of the things you would love to achieve in your life if your wildest dreams were to come true, do you know that you are taking a step towards achieving those dreams? Let me explain.

Everything in this life is experienced through our thoughts. We construct our reality with our thoughts. We proved this with the first exercise, which was to have a thought, and then to notice how it affected your feelings and your body. Remember that when you thought a particular way, your entire physical experience changed to accommodate that thought. You became weighed down by low-frequency, negative feelings. 'I hate it when they … I'm useless at … Everything works against me … I'm going to make them pay…'

Confucius, the great Chinese philosopher from more than 2500 years ago, said, 'If you're going to pursue revenge, you'd better dig two graves.' He was so right – if you persist in negative thoughts, you will destroy yourself and almost certainly destroy your chances of achieving those wonderful dreams.

If you continually think limiting, negative thoughts, I promise you that your life will absolutely reflect those thoughts: you will live a limited life that is not what you want, and you will be tied to the negative, low-frequency feelings that go with such an unsatisfied life. You will feel like a victim, you will blame others for your predicament, and you will feel frustrated. I can guarantee that you will really struggle to make headway in your quest to connect with spirit. Spirit simply doesn't exist on this plane. To connect with spirit, we need to raise our energy frequency. Sounds easy! But how do we do it?

What do you think would happen if you were to change your thinking? I'm not suggesting it's as easy as changing your shirt, but it is possible. And the key is in the very first exercise that we did – the one where you become aware of your feelings at that moment.

Now I want you to take that exercise a little further. Become tuned in to yourself. Notice your thoughts. Be aware of your feelings and how they make certain parts of your body feel a certain way. Practise. Get in the habit of just checking in with yourself at random moments during the day. Ask yourself, 'How do I feel right now?' Run that torchlight of your own consciousness over your body and into your mind to explore the thought–feeling connection.

Catch yourself in the act of thinking negative thoughts! Did you experience a moment of jealousy or resentment? Do you easily take offence, believing that people too easily dismiss you and put you down? Don't beat yourself up; simply note with interest what your automatic thought has been, note the attendant feelings, and then quite consciously try and turn that thought around. Sure, this can be hard at first – a bit like trying to slam on the brakes of a freight train – but it will become easier, more automatic, with time and practice.

This is such a simple exercise to do. It requires no writing or even any 'me' time – it really can be done on the fly, many times a day.

Later, when you come to do your spiritual practice and are sitting quietly in meditation, this advanced attention to your own feelings and your own reality will greatly benefit you in your communication with spirit. Spirit is such a subtle presence that the more self-knowledge you have, the better able you will be to feel spirit's presence, and to hear the messages communicated to you.

People often ask me how they can be sure that what they're 'hearing' or 'feeling' in their minds is actually from spirit, and not just from their own imagination. One of the most important answers relates entirely to this exercise of knowing yourself. When you understand yourself and are fully aware of what it means to be you, you will be hypersensitive to messages from the other side.

Spiritually sensitive people who work very closely with other people can be in danger of getting confused about the dividing line between their own thoughts, feelings and experiences, and those of their clients or co-workers. I met a woman, Christine, who is a hair dresser. She has consciously made her salon a beautiful, peaceful space and her clients certainly feel very safe there. But as she works on their hair, obviously in constant contact with their physical body, and in contact with their aura, she picks up a lot about what's going on for them, and often she is taken quite unaware by spiritual messages for them that just come, without thought, from her mouth. 'I'll just randomly say things and then they say, "Oh my God,"' she says. 'I don't even know why I say it.'

Worse, when her clients leave, she often suffers the residue of their feelings and experiences, and becomes confused about where her own experiences end and theirs begin.

She has a lot going on, but it's not always her own stuff. Self-knowledge can help someone like Christine. Being fully conscious of her own state of mind will help her realise when she's being encroached upon by the experiences of someone else.

However, it is not enough to simply catch yourself out in the act of thinking negative thoughts. And this is where things start to get really exciting ... What if you could not only stop thinking negative thoughts, but actually start to fill your life with joy?

If you can imagine it, you can be it. Now don't get silly about this – if you imagine that you're the Queen of Great Britain, you will surely be disappointed. But if you imagine yourself as a powerful person who takes ownership of your own life – well, now you're talking!

This is called 'visualisation' and it is extraordinarily powerful. Again, it relies on your self-knowledge of how you want your life to be in order for you to activate all your positive emotions. The simple key is, don't wait for the physical world to be all that you wish it to be: use your thoughts to create the world you want. You want relationships that are more loving, respectful and harmonious? Then it's up to you to behave as if they already are. By visualising things as we want them to be, and then behaving as if they already are that way, we are doing something very powerful.

EXERCISE

The great secret is that you don't need to wait for the world to do or be as you wish: you can create the world you want. Do you wish you were a joyful, happy person? Fill your head with the message that this is what you are. Focus on that thought. Allow yourself to feel what it is like to be joyful. Cultivate the thought that you are joyful, and you will raise your energy vibration to a higher frequency. Your thoughts determine your experience.

This is the third step in the exercises I've suggested to you. Thoughts, feelings and actions are inevitable partners and will always work together in your life. Whether they work negatively or positively is entirely up to you.

And here is another wonderful truth about the power of your own thoughts to determine the colour of your life – if you cultivate negative thoughts, feelings and actions, the store of energy within you will also be negative. You will stock up on anger, resentment, fear, depression and so on. And whatever is in you, that is what you will give to the world. It can be no other way. You can only give away what you have. Along with this comes another fact: whatever is in you will attract the same qualities from the world and people around you. If you are trapped in low-energy thoughts and feelings, guess what kind of people will find their way into your life? Like attracts like.

If you cultivate positive thoughts, however, you will be putting positive energies into your internal stockroom: forgiveness, generosity, joy, gratitude. All the good things in life! And guess what: when you have these high-frequency energies in your stockroom, that's what you will give out to the world. You will find that the people and experiences attracted to you will also have those same qualities. You get back what you put out.

If you choose to make your thoughts, feelings and actions work positively through your clarity, optimism and inspiration, you will raise your personal frequency towards that of the spirit realm. You will literally come closer to spirit.

Meditation

KNOW YOURSELF

I ask for guidance to understand myself so that I can be true to myself. I ask for guidance to understand that when I am more fully aware of myself as a separate, physical being, I am coming closer to understanding that I am part of all things – that I am a spiritual being.

The following exercise takes a little more time than the previous ones. It's designed to make you more aware of the sensations within your own body – an extension of the grounding exercise above.

Sitting or lying, close your eyes and begin your practice of breathing. Don't rush this. Focus on the breaths coming into, and being expelled from, your body. As you breathe in, imagine that you are inhaling white light – purity and love. As you exhale, imagine you are breathing out all your tight negativity and daily dramas. Breathe deeply, and release.

When you feel that you have relaxed and your focus has clarified, turn your attention to your physical body. Send your thoughts, like a beam of pure consciousness, to your furthest extremity, your toes. Notice them, relax them, and move your beam of consciousness a little further up to your ankles, your calves, your knees. Acknowledge any aches or tensions, and inhale your breath of white light to that area. Move up your body – to your pelvic area, your stomach, your chest. Your consciousness is like a giant scanner. Take your time, breathing slowly and deeply into each part of your body, and feeling it release as you exhale. Move to your fingertips, your hands, your wrists, your arms, your elbows, and do the same thing. Spend some breaths on your shoulders – they carry so many burdens for us in our daily lives – your neck, head and all the little muscles in the face. You might be surprised to find just how tense you are around the mouth and eyes. Consciously send your breath of white light to your face, and feel your entire skull letting go, releasing.

In this state of hyper body awareness keep breathing for a few minutes. If you find your mind wandering, don't worry, just gently refocus on your breathing, in and out. When you feel ready to step back from this lovely state, take a minute to reorient yourself back into your physical surroundings, reminding yourself of where you are. Open your eyes.

STEP FOUR

Trust

Fear knocked at the door. Love answered and there was no one there.

–English proverb

How do you tell the difference between positive and negative energies? Positive spirit will make you feel comfortable; negative spirit will make you feel uncomfortable. While that sounds straightforward, we must treat this subject with a great deal of respect. Negative spirit is not something you want to mess around with but, having said that, if you understand how to deal with it, you do not need to feel afraid.

Have you ever woken up to find somebody in spirit standing at your bedside? You recognise them; you feel their love. You know this person! It feels as if you could reach out and just give them a big old hug. Then, bang, they're gone. It might only ever happen once, but isn't it enough? It seems it is human nature to always want more, even when we've just been offered a miracle.

You can't bring that person back; you can't force them to reappear when you want. You can ask them and be patient but you can't make them come back and get a hug, like we all wish we could. It's sad, yet you can honour what you had and you can also honour your relationship between this world and the next, and be respectful and thankful for the contact that you are blessed with.

Sometimes our experiences of spirit are not so nourishing. Like Andrew, for instance, who told us in the first chapter about his childhood experiences of feeling hands moving up his body, and things coming out of wardrobes. That would scare anybody – the same kind of thing certainly used to scare me, and made me want to close down my ability to see spirit.

It's natural to question why you would receive negative energy if it's all coming from a place of love. However, you have to understand that, as in all things, the spirit realm consists of polarity: the good, the bad; the yin, the yang – you can't have one without the other. It's the circle of life, and it sits in perfect balance.

Therefore, when we are blessed to experience spirit, to see and hear things, the dark stuff will be there too.

Initially when you connect with spirit, it's just so exciting. Your head says, 'Choice!' but what is your heart saying? Is it whispering, 'Be careful here'? Or even, 'Watch out!'?

Keeping safe with spirit is all about listening to your own heart and being alert to the messages it's sending you. Even ordinary life is like this, is it not? It's about trusting your instincts. How often have you met someone – your friend's new boyfriend, for instance – and there's just something about him you don't like? You try to like him, but something in your heart tells you that things are not quite right here. This guy is not what he seems.

Usually, this will be a message you'd rather not hear. Your friend thinks her new boyfriend is a great, caring guy, but you just can't shake the feeling – and it might be based on very little things: something about his body language, his eyes, just the feel of him, a kind of intuitive knowing – that he's shady, dodgy and would stab you in the back the moment you turned your back on him. So often these feelings are borne out, are they not? Eventually, this guy's cover will be blown, and everyone else will realise, 'Look what he's done!'

Spirit can do the same thing. Sometimes this happens to me on stage. A spirit will come through and begin chatting to me, but instead of things going smoothly, the communication quickly starts to go wrong. Spirit makes me look like a muppet, giving me wrong information, playing around, teasing me, making me feel incredibly uncomfortable. I will tell them that if they can't be honest with me then they need to go away. Sometimes I will say, 'Back off' and physically hold my hand up before them, because I need that enforcement to be there. I say, 'If you're going to mess me around, I don't want to talk to you because you're fooling me and I don't like being played like that.'

When you take charge of the situation like this, spirit will usually back away.

Spirit can also come through and not be the person they say they are. A negative energy will sometimes pretend to be somebody else. This is the dark, heavy stuff and where it gets complicated. But again, if you stick to your rules you will protect yourself. In this realm of spirit communication, things only go wrong when we don't abide by the rules, when our egos get in the way and we think we don't need to lay our basic foundation. We can ride out there like lone cowboys into danger, but if we do that, we will get into trouble.

Don't mess around; adhere to the rules. They are there for a reason.

When we open a communication with spirit, remember that we ask to be clothed in a robe of white light. This is highly protective, as spirits who are of negative intention do not like the white light and will avoid it.

It's your life, not theirs

I have had a personal experience of being taken in by spirit. It was years ago, when I had just begun harnessing my gift. I was very excited about it all – too excited to stop and listen to my heart, as it turned out. At the time, I was living in a way-cool apartment right on the lake at Rotorua. It was a place of peacefulness, and I just loved hanging out there, talking to spirit. I was meditating a lot and, despite some serious health problems, feeling calm and spiritually centred for the first time in my life.

A spirit started whispering to me that I should move house. This wasn't a spirit that I knew, but I was so excited by the whole experience of communicating in this way that I didn't stop to think. Spirit was telling me to move house? Sure, you bet! I moved – and things immediately went downhill from there. I had been so happy and grounded in my first flat; now I was back in a darker place.

I learned two big lessons from that experience. The first was: don't listen to spirit when you don't know who it is. This is why I encourage you to make connections with people that you know – your family members and very close friends; your mum, dad, grandparents. These are people with proven love for you who will not do you wrong. When that spirit told me to move house, I never once ascertained who it was. I didn't know them. Why did I listen? Because I was too excited to just be still, to listen carefully to the effect they were having on me, to lay down my basic protections, and to seek validation of who it was.

The other important lesson is this: do not let spirit run your life for you. Our wairua – our loved ones in spirit – love us and support us. They guide us, but they can't tell us what to do.

As an example, I met a woman who had landed in a real mess when she believed her grandmother in spirit was telling her to change jobs, leave her family and move away. She was so certain it was her grandmother, and she was so excited to be in communication with spirit, that she did everything she was told.

Later, she said she had an uncomfortable feeling in her heart – a little voice saying, 'I don't think so, I don't think so,' – but her head was saying, 'Yeah, let's do it because Nan said so.'

Well, she ended up in an absolute mess. She made all those changes, but did they bring her any happiness? Quite the opposite – she left a real trail of destruction in her wake.

The question here is: why would you do what somebody told you without really holding that advice up to the light of your own judgement? Do you do what you're told when living people order you around? I hope not. Why then would you unthinkingly obey spirit? Even the advice of genuinely loving spirit needs to be filtered through your own heart. We thank spirit for their advice, we thank them for their love, and then we must make our own decisions. It's our life, our path.

If we blindly take the advice of spirit and do what they say, we have no one to blame but ourselves. It's a hard way to learn that lesson. It's much easier to ask for protection at the outset, receive spirit's messages with gratitude, and then go away and truly think about what action you want to take.

Loving messages from spirit do not usually tend to be 'do this, do that' kind of messages. They are usually inspirational – they let us know we are being watched over, that our struggles are noted, and often contain positive and encouraging messages to help us strengthen ourselves so that we are better able to face our challenges.

They've lived their life already, and they can't boss you around. That's really important. Make up your own mind about what you want to do. You've only got one shot in this physical body – just one – to make this life an amazing one.

Generally, if you have created the white light environment, spirits of negative intention will not want to come into that zone.

Psychic attack

Sometimes we are attacked by negative energies at night. When I was about 15, I woke up with a terrible feeling of being suffocated. Something dark was trying to swamp me and hold me down. I couldn't breathe, move, or even scream. I didn't want to open my eyes because I was too scared. I was praying, 'Please don't let me open my eyes,' but what did I do? I opened my eyes, and I saw the darkest thing I've ever seen in my life, smothering me and trying to get into my system. It was a horrible feeling. This has happened to me many times since, and I've learned that if I ask my grandfather – who is one of my spirit guides, and someone I totally trust – he will come and push them away.

These occurrences – which we call 'psychic attack' – are perhaps a reflection of our fear within our lives. They usually come during times of trouble, when our personal frequencies are low and we are beset with the challenge of negative emotions. When we feel like that, there is not much room in our psyche for white light connection, and dark spirits can more easily find their way in.

But the attacks can also come when you are making spiritual progress and becoming more attuned to the universe – as if darkness can't bear for you to go further into the light.

There's no doubt that psychic attack is horrible and very frightening. You need to keep calm, and call for the help of your loved ones in spirit. Most of all, you need to pray. I find the Lord's Prayer very effective. Just keep repeating it until you feel safe, and do not stop praying until that dark presence goes.

The Lord's Prayer

This simple but powerful prayer has come down to us through the Bible, in which it was said to come from Jesus himself. It is a wonderful prayer when you need protection from negative forces, and I also use it as a focusing prayer. I say it line by line, repeating until I am fully in tune with the words and their meaning. Sometimes, if I'm getting interference from thoughts or other disruptive energies, I need to repeat it several times until I am clear of distraction and ready to proceed with my meditation or whatever I'm doing.

> Our Father who art in heaven,
> Hallowed be thy Name.
> Thy kingdom come.
> Thy will be done,
> On earth as it is in heaven.
> Give us this day our daily bread,
> And forgive us our trespasses,
> As we forgive those who trespass against us,
> And lead us not into temptation,
> But deliver us from evil.
> For thine is the kingdom,
> And the power, and the glory,
> For ever and ever.
> Amen.

We were talking about this at one of my workshops when a woman named Melanie shared her experience of being visited by negative energies – and her very unusual way of dealing with them.

'When I'm going to sleep,' she said, 'I quite often have a problem with energies that come out at night, and I can't seem to get rid of them. I fight them and sometimes I do a couple of karate kicks at them.'

Everyone cracked up when she said that, and I said, 'I hope you don't miss them and hit your husband!'

She replied, 'I find that I can cope with a lot of different energies but sometimes ones that come in at night are much stronger. I used to be afraid, but now I get up and fight them and tell them to go away.'

I suggested that it was being startled that made her defensive.

She agreed that was true. 'During the day I can control it. I can put a white light around me and flush out the house. I do it at nighttime but they still seem to get through. And obviously when I'm asleep I don't like it, because I feel I'm not controlling what's going on. Sometimes it might just be a nice guy that's passing through who wants me to say hi to someone or other. But for some reason when I'm asleep, that's when the negative energies come and I don't know how to deal with them.'

'Why do you think they're negative?' I asked.

'Because they feel dark,' she answered.

I thought I understood what was going on. 'Basically, when we go into that sleep zone or at nighttime, we can be psychically attacked but we can also just be the receptor of unwanted but not necessarily malicious visits, too. We need to remember that when we are attuned, others will come along with the ones we've actually invited.

'Instead of running away from them and kicking them and all that, it's better just to stand and say, "Hey guys, look, I'm just having a sleep." You can do it in your head. I believe you're fighting them when you don't need to. You just need to let them go through.'

I offered a prayer of protection for Melanie's house: 'We ask that Melanie's house be wrapped in white light, from all four corners, from top, bottom and sides. We ask that anything negative that walks through her house, especially when she's sleeping, to please cease doing this and to go another pathway. We ask that she be allowed to be at peace when she sleeps, in harmony with the universe instead of fighting in her sleep. We ask that her pain be released so that she no longer needs to carry it for everybody else. We ask that this protection be granted now and we ask that her friends and family that love and support her in the spirit world will watch her and protect her and keep anything negative away from her.'

Footprints in time and space

Sometimes the dark things that we experience are not spirits, but the residue of past events, or of people who used to live in that house or area. I'll give you an example.

I was driving along the road with a pedestrian crossing ahead of me, when suddenly an old woman stepped out onto the road. She seemed to come out of nowhere – a down-at-heel woman, carrying a number of old bags. I slammed on my brakes and skidded to a halt, but there was no way I could have missed her. As the car stopped, my heart was banging and I was filled with horror. I leapt out of the car and went running around to see what I'd done. There was no sign of the lady. I checked under the car, over the car, on the side of the road in case she'd been thrown – nothing. I was badly shaken but I got back in the car and drove to where I was headed, just up the road. When I got there, I told my mate what had happened.

'Oh, yeah,' he said, not looking very surprised. 'There was an old bag lady killed on that crossing a week ago by a truck.'

So, what I had seen was the residue of that accident. It hadn't been the woman's ghost, but just a residual energy of what had happened there. It's the same kind of residual energy that is often present in houses – you know, that feeling you get when you go into a house and you feel uncomfortable, usually because there has been a lot of conflict there.

If you have a child who is often afraid at night, it could be because they are spiritually sensitive and pick up on the residues of people and events from the past – negative things that happened in their bedroom a long time before. It could also be a spirit just trying to torment the child because it knows they're gifted.

Just like in ordinary life, where there is always a balance – a polarity of good and bad, yin and yang, male and female – so there is in the spirit world a polarity between light and dark. We often talk about the vortex of white light – well, the opposite of that is the vortex of negativity. The best way of describing them is that they're like little time tunnels – tunnels of negative energies that flow through from spirit world to this one. Spirits come to disrupt us, to toy with us, to play with us.

We have to understand about the polarities so that we can learn to tell the difference. It all comes down to really tuning in to yourself. But, becoming aware of these possibilities should not distract us from wanting to connect with spirit. These are risks, but they're risks we can deal with through self-knowledge, devotion to spiritual practice, and adherence to the rules of safety.

Nigel Collis – clairvoyant and spiritual cleanser

A good friend of mine, Nigel Collis, is a clairvoyant, healer and medium. He is a super talented spiritual healer who believes in the higher power of white light, the love of Christ and the beauty of the masters, as I do. He heals people and, with a group of other spiritually gifted people, clears houses of residue, negative energy and dark spirits.

People have different kinds of spiritual connection and strengths, he says, and that's why he always works with a group of five or six.

'Different people pick up different things which all add to what we find in the home,' he says. 'Someone might pick up the energy of a child, and others might pick up the child's mother. It's very intertwining and it helps build on the story of what's happened in the home or around the home. Also, depending on circumstances, things can be quite heavy, making it safer to be in a group. Perhaps the former occupants of a house have dabbled in witchcraft, or been into drugs – both those things leave behind some dark and frightening energy.'

In my own home, Nigel's group picked up on some dark energy in a corner of one room and realised that the previous occupant had sat right there at his computer, surfing the internet for porn. It's so good to be able to clear away such heavy residues.

Nigel always begins with the Lord's Prayer, then a protection prayer for the people taking part in the cleansing or clearing, and then he calls on the masters for guidance.

'Every house cleaning is different,' he says. 'Sometimes the earthbound spirits don't want to go to the light, and we don't stop till they go through. When we clear a property we open a vortex of white light above the home and leave it open for a specified number of hours. This allows negative energies and all people in that area who don't know they've died to move through. By doing this, we also clear the surrounding properties.

'Everybody who takes part is clairvoyant, so whatever comes through them will be used to clear the space. Some people use lavender water to help cleanse the area. Sometimes, if it's Maori residues or issues, we might have to give some greenstone back to the land. Sometimes the house may be affected by curses; however this is unusual. Most homes have just been affected by negative energies.'

And at the end of the process, Nigel says, it's really important to close down properly. 'We thank God for allowing us to come into the home. And we do a blessing to keep the house clear and keep the occupants safe and relaxed.'

The healing that Nigel does is really cool. I recommended a friend visit Nigel after she lost a child. Now, please don't go thinking that people like Nigel and I can simply remove grief – of course we can't and we wouldn't want to, as it's a normal part of life. But spiritual healing is about strengthening a person's spirit so that they are better able to deal with the difficult things in their life.

My friend told me, 'I felt so calm after seeing Nigel. I'm definitely better about handling my grief. I can cope. The healing definitely worked for me, and I'm so grateful to him for giving me this sense of hopefulness.'

Says Nigel, 'The secret of being a good healer is humility – to be humble because it is not you, but God's energy working through you.'

Nigel can be contacted through his Auckland shop Health World. If you live out of Auckland he will probably be able to recommend someone to clear your house in your own area. However, he also does absent clearing – from New Zealand, he has cleared houses in England, South Africa and Australia. Nigel's contact details are at the back of this book.

Fear stops you following your heart

The old English proverb at the top of this chapter perfectly describes how we overcome our fears: 'Fear knocked at the door. Love answered and there was no one there.' It's also sometimes expressed: 'Fear knocked at the door. Faith answered and there was no one there.'

Either way, it's a beautiful idea: that our love – which is our connection with spirit, the purest form of love – or our faith in spirit, will protect us from all fear. This is true when we're talking about the really dramatic forms of psychic attack, but it's just as true when we consider the other common forms of fear that beset us in our daily lives, and which hold us back from developing spiritually.

Fear embodies what I call the low-frequency energies – all the negatives such as hate, resentment, anger and so on. It closes us down, traps us inside our lives and keeps us in a state of non-exploration and non-risk. It shrinks us!

Its opposite is love, which embodies the high-frequency energies of joy, generosity, gratitude and peacefulness. Love opens us up into both our daily world and the boundless universe. It allows us to push our own boundaries. It expands us!

Whichever fear is the biggest problem for you – whether it's fear of the unknown, fear of loneliness, of disapproval, or the biggies such as fear of failure and fear of death, it will contain one essential truth: it is the thing that stops you following your heart. Imagine if you had no fear. What could you do? What could you not do?

If you were to follow your heart's desire, what is the worst thing that could happen? Are you afraid that you would fail? Let me tell you something: failure does not exist. How can we fail in God's perfect world? We might not achieve what we set out to achieve, but nevertheless we won't fail if we learn from the experience and remain cheerful and positive. Experience is what gives us our wisdom – and how can the gaining of wisdom ever be classified as failure?

Do you think I'm playing mind games with you? I am certainly suggesting that you use your mind on this, but there's no trickery involved – just a new way of looking at the world.

Look at it this way. You hold inside you all sorts of dreams for a life that's different to the one you have now. Perhaps you want to change your career, or go on an adventure, or learn a new skill – or learn to communicate directly with spirit. All these dreams are fabulous. How can they not be? They are the true messages of your heart.

But we often ignore our dreams. We tell ourselves not to be silly, that we might fail, that we don't deserve such achievements.

As humans we have been blessed with an incredible brain. What an amazing combination of abilities we have! Yet that left side of our brain can cause us problems if we let it dictate the terms of our life. How about listening to the right side of your brain – dare to dream, and then let your left side help you figure out the steps you need to take to achieve your goal. This is so important.

Again, it is the right side of your brain that will let you know your true feelings about what you're doing. If you take the time to stop and listen to yourself in the midst of your busy life, as you do in meditation, perhaps you might detect frustration, irritation, even sadness. This is such a good indication that you are not being true to yourself and your heart. Stop, and let those feelings tell you what is really going on. Those feelings will provide the key to the really big questions about how you actually want to live your life. Your feelings are very powerful, and it's up to you whether that power works for good or bad in your life. You can create your own prison through feelings and negative thoughts; or you can set yourself free by allowing your feelings to take you to a more positive life.

What makes you happy? Your heart will tell you. The worst thing would be to be on your deathbed full of regret and doubt – to wish you'd done something else, but it was too late. Isn't it worth facing your fears, replacing them with love and faith, in order to avoid that terrible scenario? We are only in this physical body once. It is your responsibility to do it well.

When you take the time to connect with spirit, the white light will shine straight into your soul and reveal your own truth.

That is the time to trust spirit. It's also the time to go back to spiritual basics: to ask for protection, to allow yourself to safely trust what you feel. Trust and focus.

Journey to spirit

GLEN

The experience of a young man I met at one of my workshops perfectly encapsulates much of what I'm saying here. He became aware of spirituality when he was about 10. A friend's mother was heavily into spirit – or 'ghosts' as most of the other children thought. But the friend told Glen that he had an ability in this area. All Glen remembers, though, is that he had many scary dreams as a child and many nights sleeping with his parents or brother, too scared to go to his room.

He has an interesting theory about why children are so susceptible to spirit, and why so many psychics trace their experiences back to early childhood.

'Maybe,' he says, 'it's because their minds are not full of anything. They have no beliefs, no deep thoughts, no entrenched ideas about the way life is or is to be. Spirit can then connect to this free mind. As adults, and especially in this time of busy lifestyles, we get so flustered and overwhelmed with our day-to-day activities that we forget to slow down and appreciate the simple and loving parts of life.'

As a child he went to church, but after his father died when Glen was 15, he became very negative towards religion and the afterlife. 'How come good people are taken early? I didn't think that was fair. The pastor at the time said it was about faith but I wanted "real" answers, of which none were forth-coming. I became a realist. If it wasn't in front of me, it wasn't true.'

Then, when Glen was in his early thirties, he saw the English medium Colin Fry on TV and was very impressed. To Glen, what he saw constituted 'proof' – as I also believe it to be – that there is an afterlife and a Creator.

'From then on,' Glen says, 'I had a strong desire to witness this in person and to pursue this area.'

Glen is a very intuitive person, and is blessed with the gift of seeing auras. He says he saw a large purple aura around me, but more often sees white ones around people. He also has healing hands: when he put his arm around my shoulders in order to have a photo taken, I felt the painful tension in my muscles easing. He was surprised when I told him this, but he agreed he has a great feeling of energy within himself that he likens to the feeling you get when you hear the haka in full cry and get goosebumps all over – soul energy.

Returning home from one of my workshops, he says he was really excited.

'I had to try this technique of sitting in a quiet space, somewhere I felt safe. I had a candle lit and did my affirmation asking for protection and requesting spirit to come forward. I was in a relaxed state and felt positive. After a while nothing had happened so I thought I would try again another time.

'Later that night I awoke to see an elderly gentleman standing near the doorway of our bedroom. He was very clear to me and I knew he was not a burglar. He wandered around a bit then looked at me before disappearing. I thought this was great but my wife was a little scared of what I was saying and what was happening.

'It only happened one other time, again at night, perhaps because I'm in a state of peace and my mind is not full of things. A lady appeared on my bed. She looked very distressed and had her head lowered as if she was in shame about something. Her face was withered and she was not happy at all. I asked her who she was but again she just disappeared.'

Since these two connections Glen has tried numerous times to connect with spirit but without any joy.

'I get angry at not being able to connect,' he says, voicing the frustration of many people who struggle to find this clarity of connection. 'I wonder if I did something wrong. Am I not a good enough person to connect with spirit? I keep doing the same ritual as before – but nothing. You get frustrated and give up for a while, then you see a wonderful story on TV or are part of a wonderful event in life and you want to try again. I consider myself to be luckier than most as at least I've had that experience of seeing spirit.'

He says he will keep trying and would like to attend a spiritual church. Whatever happens, he says this spiritual journey has helped him immensely. I believe that if Glen can learn to recognise and deal with his intense expectations, he will develop a happier and more satisfying relationship with spirit. It is his spiritual practice that will take him on this journey to inner acceptance.

'I was a late bloomer in the sense of knowing who I am as a person. We all chase ideals and expectations but at some point in life you must find peace as to what you have, what makes you happy and what's left that you need to do before your bath water runs out and you pass over. We can all get stuck in the way we think, the jobs we do and the outlook for ourselves. I'm much happier and more positive knowing there is another

Meditation

OPENING THE THIRD EYE

The chakras are energy centres within the body. I think of them as being like psychic organs that produce and distribute energies throughout our being. There are about a hundred little chakras that we usually call meridians. Even in Western culture, we're getting used to the idea of these ones, as they are what are used during acupuncture, and are to do with our physicality.

However, the seven primary chakras deal with emotions and spirituality.

The Crown chakra is located at the top of the head, and is to do with understanding, cosmic consciousness and enlightenment.

The Third Eye chakra is located at the middle of the forehead, and is to do with clairvoyance, visualisation, psychic senses and pictures.

The Throat chakra is to do with communication, creativity and healing.

The Heart chakra is to do with love, hope and compassion.

The Solar Plexus chakra is to do with energy, vitality, desire and power.

The Sacral chakra is located below the bellybutton and is to do with emotions, sexuality and intimacy.

The Root chakra is located at the base of the spine and is to do with survival instinct, security and grounding.

The third eye, also known as our inner eye, lies dormant in most people. However, if you wish to develop your spiritual awareness and to communicate with spirit, you will need to develop your third eye, as it is with this chakra that we see beyond the physical and receive visions and messages from spirit.

To open your third eye, create your usual safe place in which to meditate. You will also need a candle for this meditation.

I ask for protection, and also for clarity and insight. I ask for spirit to help me in my quest for spiritual awareness, and I ask for the strength to deal with whatever I may be shown.

Light your candle and sit before it. This meditation is a little more difficult than the previous ones, as this time you are not going to close your eyes. Do your breathing, and allow your eyes to rest on the candle. The candle's flickering is very focusing for this exercise, and will help you trigger your third eye.

While you are looking into the candle, focus your energy – your visualisation – between your two physical eyes. Keep breathing, in and out. Totally relax your physical eyes and send your attention inwards to your third eye, visualising that spot between your eyes, above the bridge of your nose. You may start to see a speck of light in the distance and if you do, allow all your focus to rest upon it, while breathing into it. Do remember that this can take time. I liken it to the life cycle of a butterfly – it takes time for a beautiful Monarch butterfly to emerge from its chrysalis, and this is the same sort of process.

Imagine there is a curtain over your third eye, and you are opening it.

The more you repeat this exercise, the easier it will become for you to connect with your third eye. As you breathe, become aware of the energy field around you. Notice any warmth that may be present around your head, face or at the back of your neck. This warmth can indicate a presence coming within your aura, attracted by the energy you are creating. You don't need to do anything; just notice the warmth and keep calmly breathing and focusing.

This is an incredibly powerful spiritual tool.

When you are ready to stop, shift the intensity of your focus away from your third eye, and begin once again to notice the physicality of the candle, and then of the room around you. Don't rush this period of re-orientation. It's important to feel very integrated and grounded back into yourself before you end your meditation. Your prayer of closure and thanks to spirit will greatly help you re-enter your ordinary senses again.

STEP FIVE

Surrender past hurts

Spirit is the sword and experience the sharpening stone.

–Arabian proverb

Life does not always run smoothly and sometimes we face times of intense challenge. At times like that I am reminded of poor old Job – the dude in the Bible whose faith in God was tested again and again. He lost all his worldly possessions, his children were killed and all sorts of other calamities befell him – including boils! The story goes that Job was a very pious man, but Satan told God that Job was only pious because he was so lucky in life. Satan reckoned that if Job fell on hard times, he would quickly turn away from God. So, all of Job's tribulations were part of a mighty contest between God and Satan, to see whether Satan could get Job to curse God's name. But Job never did. Instead, he said things like, 'The Lord gave and the Lord has taken away. Blessed be the name of the Lord.'

How many of us greet our misfortunes with such equanimity? And yet it's true that every challenge, every obstacle that's put in our path, is an opportunity for us to grow. Okay, it might not seem like it at the time, but most steps towards spiritual understanding are taken as a result of facing and dealing with tough times.

From personal experience, I can tell you that when I have faced terrible life events, such as being badly injured as a child, or the end of a relationship, I, like anyone else, have felt terror, anger, frustration – in a word, devastation. At times like that, it is hard to see your true path in life. There is a reason why tragedy is often described as 'soul destroying'.

Sometimes you let people into your life who end up eroding your self-confidence and your security. They take from you, but give nothing in return except coldness. I typify these people as 'spiritual vampires' as they suck the spiritual essence from you, betraying the trust and friendship you have offered them.

Other times, it's simply that life deals us tragedy – the loss of a child, the loss of our home, a serious illness or accident, a major disappointment of some kind.

How do we deal with this kind of thing? I don't want to be glib about this, or belittle just how hard it can be, but the truth is that we have to go back to the basics of spiritual practice, and our sense of who we are.

Often when we face serious setbacks, we become bitter and angry. We may feel that life is unfair, that God is unjust or does not exist. Our negativity ties us to the traumatic event, and we drag all that pain along with us into the future.

It's important to realise that these reactions are choices that we make. Understandable, maybe, but still a choice, and not one that will help us in the long run. When life throws us challenges, as it will do, we decide how we will respond. Hardships are always a spiritual challenge: will you shrink or grow? Will you turn away from spirit or move closer?

This is why I love the quote that opens this chapter. It has so much wisdom in it: out of our harshest times can come our most profound spiritual discoveries. If we had the choice, we would not choose the terrible things that happen to us; but can we grow from them? Can we take awful things and make them into gold? No doubt at all.

The sombre dance of grief and love

KIRSTEN

Losing a child is particularly cruel. I've seen cases where the grief has sent parents down a path of self-destruction and anger, but I've also seen parents who have turned their grief into a force for good, so that the love they have for their child is manifested in the world in a positive way.

I was at a show one night when I began to feel quite breathless. I felt as if I had a mask over my face, with tubes going into my mouth. I realised I was experiencing the sensation of asthma, and my attention was directed to a young woman sitting in the audience. 'What's your association with asthma and The Asthma Foundation?' I asked her. There was immense sadness as I realised that she had lost a young son to asthma. His name was Logan and he was four when he died, less than a year before.

Logan had been such a special little boy. 'He was a character – so vibrant, constantly busy. He never walked, he always ran,' his mother Kirsten told me. 'He had something special about him, and later we wondered whether that was because he was going to be taken so young. He was very empathetic and was lovely to other children. He made everyone laugh. He was funny and outgoing and lovely.'

Logan suffered asthma from when he was around two years old, and it was getting worse. His parents were trying to deal with it and had had the asthma nurse out just the day before he died but, Kirsten says, 'I don't think we knew enough to really get on top of it.'

Since his death, Kirsten has thrown herself into the work of Asthma New Zealand, helping raise awareness about the disease. She formed a 34-strong team, Team Logan, to compete in a half marathon to raise money for asthma awareness. 'Even after my little man's gone, he's still doing good,' she says, proudly. Logan is the poster-boy for Asthma New Zealand.

'Out of something that rocked our world and completely shook everything we'd ever believed in, from something so tragic we needed something good to come out of it, we've chosen this road. Because he was such a happy wee boy, we wanted to make him proud.'

Logan was not a sick child, and no one thought for a minute that he would die of an asthma attack. Yet he stopped breathing when he was in the car with his mother, older sister and younger brother. Kirsten drove as fast as she could to the hospital, but attempts to revive him failed, and it turned out that, unknown to everybody, Logan had a virus in his system which, combined with the asthma, caused cardiac arrest.

Looking back, Kirsten wonders if Logan knew he was not going to be with his family for long.

'My mum passed away when Logan was 10 months old and, although he never really knew her, he always said he remembered her and he always had a thing about how much he missed her. I'd say, "Yes, Mummy does too," and we'd have a chat. But one time he said, "I need to go and see Nana, Mummy." And I said, "No, you don't. You get to stay with Mummy." And he said, "No, we'll be up on the clouds watching you." That was about a month before he died.

'And then he said to me about a week before he died, "Do we die with our eyes open or our eyes closed?" So in hindsight, perhaps he did know. I think my mum was looking after him.'

Of course, I didn't know any of that, but I certainly felt the presence of a woman I took to be Kirsten's mother. 'Your mum's there too?' I asked her, and she said yes, so I knew the older woman was taking care of her grandson.

I was getting a strong image of butterflies, and this was meaningful to Kirsten, who not only had been given a butterfly in memory of her son, but who said that in the two weeks after Logan's death a butterfly on the wall in her daughter's room kept falling to the floor for no apparent reason. 'At the time we thought maybe it was Logan, and that he was saying hello to us,' she said. 'So that butterfly association is very poignant for us.'

Then I asked, 'What's this about the sandpit?'

Kirsten said that the sandpit was Logan's favourite thing in the world at kindy – there's now a rock in their sandpit in his memory. Logan's dad Dean had promised to build Logan a sandpit in their home garden, but Logan died before it was built. At the time of our reading, Dean was building it for Logan and his brother and sister.

'You can see this from your kitchen window, can't you?' I asked her. She agreed that she could.

'When you stand there looking at the sandpit and you imagine Logan playing in it, he'll be there,' I told her. I think this is very important to realise:

that she would not need a medium to help her connect to her son. When she thought about him, he would be there. Her love for him would make the connection.

I had an image of Logan hugging his cuddly, and, through me, he told his mother, 'I'm still feeling your love, Mum.'

'It was what we needed,' Kirsten told me later. 'The reading cemented to us that there is something out there, that Logan is around and we're not alone – and that helps us a lot with our healing. It's not exactly like a weight's been lifted from us, because I don't think that could ever happen, but it's a comfort. It's comforting to know that he's still around, that he sees the things we do in his memory.'

She and Dean have begun meditating, making time in their lives for the connection with spirit.

During the reading, I had a sense that Kirsten was a tangible kind of person – that it would help her to have a physical symbol of her son for her to carry with her, such as a tattoo. She told me later she was gobsmacked when I said that. 'Just a week or two before, Dean and I had discussed getting a tattoo to remember Logan. We're not tattoo people at all. But you were so right: I need something very tactile to remind me of Logan. My symbol for him is a heart, so perhaps Dean and I will get hearts tattooed to remind us.'

Kirsten and Dean had a very upsetting experience when they heard through someone else that a medium believed Logan died to teach them a lesson.

'What kind of lesson do we need to be taught to have our baby taken away from us?' Kirsten quite rightly asked.

I believe that we choose our lives here on earth – that we've sat with the Creator and mapped out our life journey. But I certainly don't believe that spirit harshly subjects us to lessons that we somehow 'ought' to learn. That makes it sound like we're naughty schoolchildren needing to be taught a lesson!

I believe that the only lesson in such tragic losses is what we have to learn in order to carry on with our lives. Tragic things happen in life so that, as Kirsten has said, everything we believe in is thrown up in the air and we have to make very hard decisions about how we will carry on. Kirsten and Dean have decided to carry on with love. That love brings them closer to the spirit of their little boy, and keeps their family intact. These things are never easy and I find it absolutely inspirational that, even in grief, people can find it in their hearts to give to others. That is what spirit is all about. In such love we find hope for the future.

When we forgive, we free our hearts

I have met many people who have, in effect, allowed themselves to become victims of their personal histories. You will have met people like this, too: unable to move on from childhood trauma, or something bad that happened, maybe years before.

Dr Wayne Dyer is a well-known author of meditation and self-development books, as well as some wonderful meditation CDs that I've found very helpful. He provides a really fantastic image of our relationship with the past. He asks us to think of a boat's wake – the frothy path that lies behind a boat as it surges forward. He points out that the wake does not drive the boat – that happens because of the present energy generated by the engine, or the wind in the sails. The analogy with life is obvious, don't you think? What lies in the past is but a trail, as insubstantial as a shadow: it cannot possibly drive us forward. And yet, so often, we let it.

I find this idea incredibly empowering, because what he's saying is that we are not slaves to the past – unless we choose to be. Remember how we were talking, in step three, about the power of our thoughts? This is another area in which we are truly powerful in our own lives, if only we give ourselves permission to be. We can choose how we will be.

If anyone can make us feel as if our soul has been destroyed, they have gained control over us. How did they do this? The only possible answer is that we let them. And if we let them into our lives, we can also decide they no longer have any place with us.

How do we do this without becoming bitter and carrying resentment around? Because let me tell you, even if you cease contact with someone who has hurt you, if you still harbour corrosive feelings about that person, they are still with you. How do we let go of these negative attachments? The answer is, I believe, one of the great spiritual mysteries: forgiveness. Yes, that's right. It is the path to peace.

Why should we forgive someone who has hurt us, you ask? Well, therein lies the great mystery. When we forgive someone, when we truly open our heart to that person, we let go of their hold on us. Forgiveness is indeed a powerful weapon. As Mahatma Gandhi said, 'The weak can never forgive. Forgiveness is the attribute of the strong.'

If we can forgive someone, we free our hearts. With forgiveness, resentment, anger and pain melt away. It is truly the most powerful form of love there is. Many of my spirit readings end up being about forgiveness. It is terrible when someone passes with words unspoken, and past wrongs unforgiven. People find it very hard to move on with their lives. And, of course, the hardest thing of all can be to forgive ourselves when we have wronged someone.

There's no simple answer to this. I have seen many cases where a person has been forgiven by the person they have wronged, and yet still can't forgive themselves. The answer is to use your spiritual practice of prayer and meditation to get close to spirit, to feel the pure love of spirit, and to release your feelings of self-blame. No, you can't change the past, but nothing is achieved by dwelling negatively upon it. It's far better to forgive yourself and replace your useless self-blame with a positive action in the present. Forgiveness does not change the past, but it does enlarge the future, as the Dutch scientist Paul Boese put it so well.

EXERCISE

This is a lovely exercise that I use when I'm struggling with negative feelings.

You need to find a place to sit where no one is going to see you. Choose somewhere nice, like the beach or the bush – somewhere without distractions. You will also need to find a few rocks and put them in a pile where you are going to be sitting.

Take some deep, peaceful breaths. Allow yourself to relax in this beautiful place that you've chosen. Then actually give yourself permission to let some of your negative preoccupations drift into your brain. Try and take each thought one at a time. Acknowledge each thought, and then surrender it to the universe.

And as you do that, pick up one of those rocks beside you and physically throw it away. You might say something like, 'I surrender my past hurt with my ex-husband.' You might then pick up another rock and this time you might be able to say, 'I forgive my ex-husband.' Allow yourself to feel the lightness you are creating in your soul through these actions.

EXERCISE

This is also a very good exercise, similar to the one above, but this can be done anywhere, even at home, as long as you can be sure you won't be interrupted – and as long as you are careful!

You will need a pen, a sheet of paper, an envelope and some matches. Again, take the time to set a good foundation: allow yourself to become peaceful and open to spirit. Now, take your pen and, giving yourself permission to let anything negative that's bothering you persistently to come into your mind, write it all down on the paper. Feel the negative emotions as you write so that they are transferred onto the page. When you have finished, seal the paper inside the envelope, and take some time to calm yourself. This can be a very emotional exercise. Allow yourself to feel the release of all that negative emotion. Then, making sure you are in a safe place – perhaps outside, or at a fireplace – light the envelope and watch it burn, saying, 'I surrender my past hurts, and release them to the universe. I allow peace and harmony to take their place in my soul.'

We all need forgiveness

Sometimes when spirits come through for someone I will perceive that one of the spirit presences is slightly apart from the others. A spirit will come through separately like that because that is how they were in life – maybe physically separate from their family, but more often it's an indication of the emotional state of the family relationships. Sometimes, this person was a negative influence on the family in some way – perhaps an abuser to his wife or children. These people eventually pass, and then in the healing space of the spirit they begin to realise the negative impact of their behaviour, and they feel regret and often want to make amends. They seek forgiveness, and at last they are open to the love that they rejected during their time here on earth.

We will all have the opportunity to see how we've lived. None of us are perfect, and we may all need forgiveness, to a greater or lesser extent. My message, and the message of most of the spirits who come back, through love, to visit their loved ones here on earth, is: wouldn't it be better to access that love and forgiveness while you're still here? Go and apologise; reshape your life so that you are sustaining, not hurting, the people you have chosen to stand next to in this life. That is the path to happiness on this earthly plane.

Three sisters came along to a show one night. Their mother had passed a couple of years before and

I could tell that they all had complicated feelings about the loss. They had all loved their mother, and yet they had residual feelings of sadness and even resentment towards her.

Their mother was there with them in spirit, and I immediately told them, 'She's making me feel as if she's softened up. She was quite firm around the edges. She's more relaxed now.'

That was the feeling I was getting – of a hard person who had softened – and as I spoke the women all looked at each other with tears in their eyes.

'She could be very hard sometimes,' one of the women agreed. 'She was always telling us to bugger off. She was a hard person to show love to.'

As she spoke, there was a crash on stage and, for no apparent reason, my whiteboard fell over. As you can imagine, the audience shouted in surprise, and the three sisters clutched each other, absolutely certain it was their mother who had pushed it.

When things settled down, I was quiet for a moment, letting the woman in spirit give me the message she wanted for her daughters. 'She knows she kept a lot in the cupboard,' I told them. 'But please note that she is very grateful for the care you gave her when she was ill, and for the love that you've always carried for her. She is sorry she wasn't more able to show her love to you, but be assured she loves you all very much.'

The sisters all had tears running down their faces. This message of love and reassurance from their mother was exactly what they had all most wanted to hear. Because of the mother's acknowledgement of the hurt she had caused, her daughters were ready to forgive instantly.

Getting free of earthly baggage

Hopefully, we learn lessons while we're here on earth. After we pass, we have a further chance to reflect on our earthly life and to learn from our experiences.

In a similar story, a woman in one of my audiences was delighted when her mother came through in spirit. The mother was very happy, thrilled to be talking to her daughter, and she had some good news, 'I've changed my way of thinking about Dad,' she said. 'I'm not grumpy with him any more!' You see? We really don't retain our earthly judgements and pettiness once we pass into spirit. Once we can forgive, we break that endless cycle of resentment and retaliation.

People often ask me if we're happy in heaven. Of course we are, because we no longer carry our load of baggage. We're free to make our peace with ourselves and our loved ones, and when we're at peace, we are happy. What a shame we can't achieve enough of that in our earthly lives.

The baggage that we cart around with us is not always our own. Often we find ourselves worrying about our loved ones and sometimes they overburden us with their expectations. This is a particular challenge: how do we remain loving and caring, without accepting a burden that is not ours to carry?

During another reading, the message that came through for the client, a woman called Helen, was very clear: 'You're not responsible: it's her decision, her life, you can't be responsible for her actions.'

Spirit was referring to Helen's relationship with her younger sister, a troubled woman who had several times tried to commit suicide, and who always needed Helen to rescue her from whatever mess she was in. Helen never managed to say no to her sister, even though various people had told her just what spirit was now telling her: she was not responsible.

Does this sound harsh? The truth is, there are people who I would class as spiritual vampires – whose needs know no bounds, and who never consider the load they are placing on others. These people need to learn personal responsibility – it is their journey, their pathway, and we must learn that we're not actually helping them when we continually bail them out of their messes.

Helen told me later that she had been given this message by friends, but somehow when she heard it from spirit, it all just clicked. The message came at the end of a moving reading, and so she was feeling spiritually wide open. As she explained, 'Something just clicked. I heard you. I listened and I heard you.'

Helen didn't just listen, she took action. She organised a meeting with her sister, and was very loving but very honest with her. She told her, 'You have no idea how heavily this weighs on me. I want to have a normal relationship with you. I want to talk about normal sister things, lovely things, not terrible things.' Helen told her that she loved her and would be there for her, but that she couldn't fix things for her.

'I was so afraid of saying those things, but I felt so much better, as if a huge burden had lifted from me. If you haven't been through that with someone so close to you, you don't understand the responsibility that you feel towards the family member. You feel so helpless.'

The next time her sister texted her, asking for money, Helen said no. She finally understood that always rushing to her sister's rescue was disrespecting herself and her own feelings, and only taught her sister to rely on her more heavily.

'I love it when things in your life put you in the path of having a better life. It's such a gift, but it's up to us to actually turn it into reality.'

We create our own suffering

At one of my workshops, a woman said that sometimes our mind can be our very own torture chamber. In this particular workshop, we were doing the final exercise, where people select an angel card and have it read for them by their partner. This woman was blown away when she selected a card that had special resonance in her own life. Her card read, 'The burden of carting your past around has made you weary, Dear One. It's time to set this burden down. Keep only the lessons and the love, and leave everything else behind. You don't want it or need it, and it's now gone.'

'What's been very helpful for me,' she said, 'is noticing that we create our own suffering. And when we're suffering, it's not what is meant for us, it's just the way we're thinking or what we're feeling. I realise, because I'm very emotional, that I have been treating my feelings as if they were facts, and that's created a lot of suffering for me. I stress, I actually stress. But the big lesson for me is that my feelings are not facts. This card is saying, "Pass it off to us, let us worry about it, let it go."'

She is so right. While it's part of our life goal to deal with what life throws at us, there are times when we create our own suffering by letting negative thoughts crowd into our mind. Recognising this is half the battle. It's all up to us. We can decide not to allow our negative emotions, our baggage, to lead us away from the light. If you're struggling with bad feelings, hand those feelings over to spirit, and feel your load lighten.

Meditation

SURRENDER NEGATIVITY

I ask spirit for guidance in surrendering past hurts inflicted on me, and to clothe myself in a robe of the white light of love and forgiveness.

Protect me from negative energies and help me to clear my mind of unpleasant thoughts and my body of negative feelings. Guide me as I embrace positive energies.

Becoming one with the universe and with spirit sounds so ultra-spiritual, but really it's just about acceptance – accepting the surroundings that you're in, the car noises, the dog barking – so that these things don't interfere with your thoughts. We become aware of everything around us; we tune in to our surrounding frequencies, and in doing that our own frequency becomes really high and sensitive to spirit.

Music is very good, and so is chanting. Many world religions use chanting to get closer to spirit. It has an incredible vibration, and it creates a real power – it gets right into your core. When it gets inside you like that it not only lifts your frequency, but allows the light to shine inside of you and disperse and dispel all the dark stuff in you.

Chanting is always done according to the vibration of the name of God. We chant using the 'Om' or the 'Aaa' because these are the sounds found within many names of God – or, more likely, God's names were born in recognition of this special vibrational tone. God Himself, Allah, Jehovah, Yahweh, Ra, Krishna.

It's not about the words; it's about the vibration coming off them. Now, you may feel uncomfortable chanting if you haven't done it before, but I want you to try it because the vibration that you create is very special, and you will feel its power.

If you don't feel comfortable doing this by yourself, you might feel better finding a meditation class. Most towns and certainly all major cities offer Buddhist centres and meditation classes. You may feel more comfortable simply attending a meditation class as there is no religious agenda – it's entirely up to you.

So, find your private meditation space and settle yourself with prayer and preliminary breathing, calming and focusing yourself on the present, feeling your way into your body, breathing in white light, exhaling your worries and fears.

Take a breath, and on the next breath out, allow your voice to activate and attach itself to the air that you're pushing out. 'Om.' Let the 'o' sound be very long – as long as your breath. Breathe in and do it again.

You might feel self-conscious or clumsy at first. Notice those feelings but reorient yourself to your breathing and keep going. 'Ooooom.'

You will certainly feel released and lighter as a God-like space opens in your head and the vibration puts you closer to the realm of spirit, of oneness.

Keep going, and when it's time to stop the chant, take time to come back to yourself. Offer a prayer of thanks to spirit for this new experience, and for allowing you to take this further step along the road to a fuller spiritual awareness.

STEP SIX

Faith

Faith is like a bird that feels dawn breaking and sings while it is still dark.

–Rabindranath Tagore,
Indian Hindu writer and mystic philosopher

If you are someone with a spiritual sensibility, life can be quite surprising at times! People often tell me they wish they could get inside my head, or see what I see – but I'm not so sure they'd really want to.

Any room I walk into is far busier for me than it is for most people – every living person usually has a spirit or two around them. In a show, the rooms can be extremely busy, with entire whanau of spirit around every living person. I used to get a shock when I was at boarding school – I would be cleaning my teeth in the bathroom, only to see a couple of strangers' faces staring at me from the mirror – maybe they were boys who had passed on, or visitors from the cemetery down the road. They'd always want to chat, but in those days I didn't understand what I was seeing, and I'd just try and block them out.

How can I tell the difference between a psychic knowing, and a spirit communication? A psychic knowing is knowledge about a person that just pops into my head spontaneously. I have no sense of it being told to me; it just is. A spirit communication, though, is where I have a sense of another being communicating information to me about someone. Being psychic is like having an intense sensitivity to the thoughts and feelings and residues of past events. However, it is something beyond the sensitivity that anyone might have towards their own loved one, where you know that person so well that you are intuitively sensitive to their subtle shifts of mood and thought. Psychic knowing of people who are strangers is much beyond reading body language. Obviously, it comes with huge ethical considerations, and I would never take advantage of someone. Going into someone's mind and reading their thoughts is unethical, and anyway, it's often inaccurate as people can have very inaccurate ideas about themselves, and don't always know what will truly be either helpful or dangerous to them. Also, when it comes to knowing the future for someone, reading their mind is not going to be any help. That knowledge doesn't come to me through thought waves! How could it? The people themselves don't know what's going to happen to them. When I see things that are going to happen, that knowledge is given to me by spirit.

It's important to note that spirit communication doesn't happen because I 'call spirits up'. I open myself up to the white light, put myself in the zone, and then spirits come if they want to. I am the conduit. It is down to their intention, not mine. I also do not channel spirit – that is, spirit does not enter my body and take me over. I am me, I am in the spirit zone, and I communicate with spirit who are separate entities to myself. It's really important to stress this point.

Early in my spiritual journey, when I was briefly in the company of somebody who was a very negative spiritual energy, I was introduced to channelling.

Channelling is when you allow spirit energy into your body, and you step out. In other words, it takes you over – what they used to call 'possession'. It's very dangerous, and can be very difficult to come back to yourself. The spirit might not want to get out of your system. It's freaky.

I met a lady once who told me, 'I have a new husband.' I thought she meant the first one had died or she was divorced, but no, it was much worse than that. She'd been married to a man named John for many years, but one day he passed out, and when he awoke he was someone different! It's what we call a 'walk in', which is when another spirit takes you over while you're still physically alive. I don't understand how it works – I have not had the experience and I never want it, but I can tell you that this lady was adamant. The man she'd been married to for 30 years was now someone with a different name, from a different world, a different time. He had a different personality, different habits, different memories – but he occupied the same body. Her husband had just disappeared.

The clutter of the past

Do you ever walk into a place and just get a feeling – perhaps a dark feeling – that something unpleasant has happened there? What you're experiencing is the residue of past events and past people, in that place. In some places it's very strong and a lot of people are sensitive to residue – or the clutter of the past.

People don't understand the effect they have on the world with their thoughts. Every thought is like a footprint in the sand. It will eventually wash away in the tide, but for quite some time it remains where you left it, swirling around, ready to be picked up by someone like me.

That's why, for me, clean and tidy hotel rooms are so important! And why some places are so difficult to be in – supermarkets, for instance, where people download all their worries and anxieties in the aisles. I have to do some serious protection work and close myself right down before I go into a supermarket, or it's too overwhelming.

While in Rome I visited the Colosseum, the site of gladiatorial games and Christian martyrs. It's still a pretty sad and intense place and I found it quite overwhelming. At first I put on my iPod and turned up the music, but I then decided it would be better to address what I was feeling and deal with it. I did a prayer, acknowledging the building's past, and I was able to deal with it much better after that.

Residue is what gave me much information when I was working on *Sensing Murder.* It's how I and the other mediums could tell where a person was killed, for instance.

In the programme about George Engelbrecht, the 91-year-old who was murdered in his own home, both Deb Webber and I were independently guided to George's house, through the back door and into the room in which he was murdered nearly 30 years earlier. I could still detect the residue lingering from the bloody attack – even though his house was now quite different. Police confirmed that both Deb and I had pinpointed the exact spot where George's body was found.

To cut a long story short, those residual sensations remain, but you have to dig through an awful lot of clutter to get to them. You've got to wade through three decades' worth to find the answer you're looking for. It can be powerful stuff. It makes you realise the value of getting your house cleansed by a spiritual healer, because all those residues of past experiences in your house will linger until you do.

What's really weird, though, is when I pick up the residue of the future. How do I know it's of the future? Sometimes I'm not sure, but mostly I can tell you that the past and future feel slightly different. The past residue feels heavy; future feels light. It's a fine line. You know how you feel the wind on your face? It's a feeling as light as that.

Here's something that happened to me that I wasn't sure how to read at the time.

I was at a friend's party and needed to visit the toilet. To get there, I had to walk past the shower cubicle and as I did so I thought, 'That's not right!' There were two guys in there, all over each other. I thought to myself, 'I've had too many beers!' So I went to the loo and on the way back I put my head down and didn't look in the shower, but nevertheless, I got it again. Aha. Residue.

But, was I seeing it as past residue or was it still to happen? I was puzzled by it, but I didn't say anything to my friend as it felt too weird. A couple of weeks later there was a knock on my door. It was my friend. She was in tears and I just said, 'Oh no.' You know what I'm going to say. She had turned up at home early from work and discovered her husband in the shower with another guy.

Sometimes residue translates in your being as emotion. You might not completely understand what it is you're encountering, but you may just feel very emotional when you walk into a place. It's not always your stuff. It's not always about you.

Places where spirit lingers

As well as the residual energies of past people and events there are places where spirits linger who, for one reason or another, have not yet crossed over. Perhaps the shock of passing was so great that they don't realise they're dead; or perhaps they don't want to be dead; or perhaps they're lost and don't know how to move into the light.

Here's a good example of this. When I'm driving, I often see figures standing next to the crosses that are put at the side of the road to show where there's been a fatal accident. These days I know what to do when I see these spirits: I acknowledge them and say a prayer and show them where the light is so that they can pass through. We call this 'soul rescue'.

I met a woman once who also sees spirits on the side of the road by the crosses. In particular, Sandy finds the Napier–Taupo highway busy with spirit, as do I, and she thinks this is partly because it's a busy and dangerous road, but also because it's an ancient thoroughfare in a part of the country that's seen a lot of Maori inter-tribal conflict in the past. The spirits she sees are not only the recently dead, but sometimes the spirits of Maori warriors; all dressed up with full tattoos, taiaha and feathers – as I did as a child from my bedroom window.

Sandy remembers the first time she saw spirit on that highway. 'It was so unexpected,' she says. 'It was night-time, and I could see a young man with a white shirt and black trousers – only I could see right through him.'

I asked her whether the young man acknowledged her, and she laughed. 'When he hopped in my car, I was sure he had noticed me!'

Luckily Sandy is good at thinking on her feet. She stayed calm and began praying. She asked for the young man to have guidance so that he could return to where he needed to be. She asked for protection for herself. 'I asked my guardian angels, I asked the Lord to grant me safety to surround and protect me. I asked my ancestors – everybody and anyone! I recited the Lord's Prayer and I asked for his family to come forward and help him on his journey – and that I be delivered safely to my loved ones.

'It was a good journey from there on, and I probably said the Lord's Prayer about six times. It's hard to explain but it wasn't until I actually felt at ease that he left the car and I could sense and see that I was on my own again.

'Now when I'm travelling along that same road I always make sure I say the Lord's Prayer and ask for protection and guidance. As a result, now when I see people, and I sense them being lost and wanting still to be here, they don't come into the car. I just say a prayer for them.'

Her experience suggests that she is conducting soul rescue for those spirits, because she has only twice seen the same spirit again. 'After I've asked that they be surrounded by their loved ones and supported to where they need to go, it's hard to describe but I do get a feeling of well-being. I don't always see them go into the light, but I have a feeling. It's very satisfying, partly because I think; right, now I can keep going! You need a good sense of humour!'

As you can see, the important thing to do when things in the spirit world take you by surprise or frighten you is to keep calm and develop a sense of control of the situation. Don't ignore spirit – there's nothing more guaranteed to keep them hanging around, pestering you. The best way to achieve peace of mind is to acknowledge them. Just say hello! Ask what they want. If you can't think what to say, prayer is always the answer – prayer is our communication with God, the Creator, spirit – it opens our connection to love, and it will always protect us.

These spirits who have not accepted their own death and who are lingering around, unsure of what to do, are automatically attracted to people who have a strong spiritual connection. It's as if we have a little beacon above our heads, and the spirits are attracted to us like moths to a flame.

Not everyone is able to stay as calm as Sandy. Another woman had much the same experience – she was driving along, and as she passed some of those white crosses she saw a man standing there, trying to attract her attention. She didn't acknowledge him and when she got home he was in her house. Understandably, some people would freak out at that point, but although it's such a surprising and vivid experience, these spirits wish us no harm. They need our help, and we can do that through our prayers, and by showing them the way to the light.

When I see them on the side of the road, I just say, 'G'day mate,' and they say, 'Oh, dude,' and next thing they'll be sitting next to me on the passenger seat.

I ask, 'Do you know what happened to you?' and a conversation will start. I say, 'This is what you've got to do: see that light over there? See those people waving? That's your dad.'

'Am I dead?'

'Yeah mate, walk, go.' It's very similar to how it's portrayed in the movie *The Lovely Bones.* Those who have passed over find their heaven when they set themselves free. Some people just don't know how to do it.

Astral travelling

While we're on the subject of things that people often find a bit freaky, let's talk about astral travel. This is where the soul actually lifts out of the body – perhaps moving just above the body, but, as you become more skilled and confident, the soul can travel to other rooms of the house, across land-scapes, into different places and even into different times.

Astral travel is another technique that has been incredibly important in the work I've done for *Sensing Murder.* I used it so that I could actually see the murderer of Angela Blackmoore. I have to say it was a very spiritually dangerous thing to do, as the darkness around such people is very frightening.

Have you ever had that experience of lying flat on your back on the floor or bed, and feeling as if you were falling? Perhaps you weren't falling – in fact, how could you have been, with a solid surface beneath you? Perhaps your soul was actually lifting upwards.

It's important to note here that, while your soul is lifting, it is still attached to you by a cord of white light – as substantial in a healthy person as a big tug-of-war rope. This is what attaches our soul to our physical body. As we grow old and close to the death of our physical body, or ill with a serious disease such as cancer or Alzheimer's, this cord becomes wispy thin as our soul's attachment to our physical body weakens. But it is not until the person actually dies that the cord is severed, the soul is released from the physical body, and can join the spirit realm.

So, while we are astral travelling, our body lies where we left it and our soul is free to travel, albeit still connected by the cord of white light to the body. There's no reason to fear it at all – it's one of the ways in which spirit will help you understand what you were put here for.

Sally often had this experience while she was asleep. She would start to lift until she had the sensation that she was flying. She found it frightening, and also threatening. I wasn't surprised, as before you take control of astral travel, it can come with a feeling of anxiety that you might not find your way back to your sleeping body.

'Yes,' Sally agreed, 'and when I wake up it feels like I'm fighting to get back in my body, and my heart's pounding and I'm really scared.'

I asked her, 'Have you ever woken up and felt as if you are drunk or hungover, yet you haven't had a drop of alcohol? You can't wake up properly; your physical body is going through the motions but you're not quite there? This is where you get a little bit stuck in between two worlds. It makes your day a bit difficult, doesn't it, because your reactions are slow, and nothing's computing.'

Sally agreed that this was just how she sometimes felt.

'Well,' I explained, 'if this happens to you and you don't take control of it, you'll wake up exhausted, unsure, confused, discombobulated. If you experience astral travelling but don't put protection on yourself, other spirits can interfere with your physical self, as if they're psychically attacking you to get into your system.'

There's a very good way to avoid such dangers. First, when you hop into bed, you visualise a bungee cord – a long, stretchy rope. Choose your favourite colour (I always choose purple). Then ask that the bungee cord be tied right around your stomach and fastened with a big bow. I ask for it to be tied to the foot of the bed in a big bow or, if I'm meditating in a chair, to be tied to the chair leg. I ask the spirits that protect me and guide me – my angels and my family – to look after me. I ask that when the lesson has been learnt for me that night, they will bungee me back safely into my room, back into my body, and I'll wake up rested, not stressed, understanding what I've experienced.

If you control your soul's journey, you build your spiritual experience and strength, and you trust the spirit to bring you back, because the bungee cord will get tighter and eventually, if it needs to, it will spring you back. You can take control of it by doing this simple exercise with the bungee cord.

You do not need to be afraid of these experiences. As long as you do your protections, you can have complete faith that your spirit guides are there to show you what you need to know. You can trust that spirit will not let you come to harm. Trust? Faith? These are very big words for those of us who might have been hurt or let down by other people in this earthly world. You might feel that trust and faith require enormous risk, but you won't know until you put yourself in the hands of spirit and allow miracles to take place.

Other spooky things

In the weird and wonderful world of spiritual connection there are a number of tools we can use to initiate or enhance our experience of spirit.

All my life, spirit tried to get my attention, but it wasn't until my early twenties that I realised this was something I could actually harness, control and use for good. When I first realised that, I went on a big learning experience, meeting other people who were interested in spirituality, and learning from them all the different ways there are to connect with spirit.

One of the first things I tried was pendulums. I was sitting with one of my new friends one night and she offered to show me how they worked. I'd always thought it was all rubbish.

'How do you know that spirit are really making these things move, and it's not the breeze?' I asked in a challenging manner.

We were sitting by the fire, and she had one of those T-shaped hangers for her poker, fire brush and pan. She pointed at the poker. 'Why don't you ask someone you know in spirit to move the poker?'

'Get out of town.'

'No, go on.'

So I did a nice little affirmation, and I said, 'Well, Poppa, if you're actually there could you move the poker?' And the blimming thing moved! It started to wobble. And I went, 'Whoa, that's freaky man, that's tripping me out. Is that you, Pop?' And it started to swing even further. Eventually it swung so much it flew off the hanger and went 'ding' onto the concrete hearth.

And I then started to test this ability even more. I said, 'Well, okay, Pop, can you move that necklace that's hanging up there?' And it moved. Then I started working with pendulums. I'd say, 'Righto, Pop, show me a yes, show me a no.'

With pendulums you start out with very basic questions, things you already know the answer to – 'Is it Friday today?' – then you can move on to questions such as, 'Is it a boy or is it a girl?'

A pendulum can be used to find things on a map, for dowsing for water and sometimes, if it feels right, to gauge somebody's health. When you're doing spiritual healing, you can wave a pendulum over someone's body and it will actually pinpoint the blockages within the system. 'What's wrong with the liver, what's wrong with the kidneys, is everything okay with the eyes?' If someone has a terminal illness, it just goes berserk.

Pendulums work on a combination of three different energies – the energy coming directly from spirit, the energy emanating from the physical object itself, and of course your own intuition. Those three things combine to help you understand.

When you're using pendulums you not only have to ask your loved one in spirit to guide you, but you must have faith in whom you're asking. You must know them and their energy so that you can trust the information they give you.

It's one of those things you have to practise and get comfortable with, and it can be very useful when you're just starting out. Pendulums are tools or vehicles to help you connect with spirit, and they can be an important part of your learning process. I don't use them any more. As I became more confident I realised it was better for me to just go straight to the source, and for many years now I have simply communicated directly with spirit.

Tarot is another one. Now, like many people with dyslexia, I'm very visual. I'm super observant, and I think in images. So the first time I saw Tarot, which of course uses images as a way of accessing spiritual truth, I was blown away. Almost literally, actually!

I was at a friend's house, and a woman pulled out a pack of Tarot cards and offered to read for another woman who was there. I'd never seen Tarot before – to be honest, I thought it sounded a bit loopy – but I asked if I could watch. She laid them out and there were all these amazing pictures, shining up at me, almost like a hologram. They beamed, they glowed, and they spoke to me. I could see a picture of a little girl holding a doll, and a story popped into my mind as if the card was talking to me. It felt like spirit was grabbing that picture and throwing it in my face. I asked if I could take over the reading.

I looked at the picture of the little girl again and estimated her to be about six or seven. I said, 'You were about six and a half when you had an experience where you were left at home alone. Your parents went out and there was no one to look after you. They neglected you. And they started to do that more frequently from six and a half years old. I know this because all I can see is you with your doll in the corner.' The woman just burst into tears, absolutely fell to pieces, because that's what took place for her.

For me it was as if a floodgate had opened.

Sometimes I might take a little minute just to ask spirit, 'Oh, what do you want me to say?' Especially when it's heavy – like molestation, domestic violence, kids being hurt in front of them and they were powerless to do anything, that sort of stuff.

So, the cards taught me how to get closer to spirit. They were leverage to get my emotions and my heart closer to spirit, because you have to know where it's coming from, otherwise you could be doing a disservice to someone.

I don't use Tarot with clients any more. I'll use them for myself and sometimes for friends, and I'll show people how to use them correctly. Tarot cards in the old days were pretty violent and evil-looking, so when somebody sees a Tarot card with a devil on it or a picture of a situation that seems evil, they can get quite freaked out, even though those pictures are just there to be interpreted. There are so many different meanings to life. But the cards I use for my guests are very positive and have all cultures in them, without judgement, from all walks of life. They're called the Voyager Tarot cards.

So, you get your cards, you sit down in your home, you light a little candle, put on some music, make everything lovely, and you ask spirit, 'Please guide me to the understanding of what you'd like to teach me today,' and you do what we call a layout.

One of my favourite layouts is the Celtic Cross. There are many variants of this, but I'll tell you the one I use. I lay down one card at the top, leave a gap and lay two below. Then I lay one to the right and one to the left, and one in the centre, thus making a cross. Then four remaining cards are laid out on the outer side of each of the points of the cross. The first six cards are about you as a person: your mental state, your emotions, your physical experience, your feminine side and your masculine side. The centre card is about your spirit. The last four cards are about what's going on in your life: your finances, your home, your work and your relationships. Each card will guide you towards understanding the parts of your life you need to change or make better.

When you get something like the death card, people say, 'Oh my God, it's the death card!' and think it means literally that someone will die. But Tarot doesn't work like that. It just means there's a beginning and an end to all things, and in this instance an end is nigh; look forward to the new beginning; let go of the old things that don't serve you any more.

Tarot is just a tool, and certainly when you're beginning to develop your spiritual skills it is a very useful one. But eventually you won't need it any more.

One thing I've never used is a Ouija board as I think they are very unsafe. People bring them out at parties, often when they've been drinking, and start trying to call up spirits. Obviously, they don't know who is going to come through, and there are no controls or protections.

I would never do any spiritual work without first asking for protection – I can't stress this enough. You just need to start by saying, 'We ask for the protection of the white light to guide us and we ask for all the negative energies and/or entities around us to be removed.' This is absolutely basic to spiritual practice.

Spiritual energies

There are two more tools that I do love to use, however – crystals and gongs. Crystals are beautiful and powerful and very useful for healing. I'm by no means an expert, but as an example, rose quartz is for peacefulness so I carry it in my pocket to feel better. Personally I look at crystals as if they're a transformer – something that absorbs energy, sustains it and holds on to it until you need to use it. When you ask for the blessing and the channelled energy to come through a crystal, it will. Then when you're done healing someone with a crystal, you give thanks and you shut it down. At the end of every healing day, I take my crystals and go down to the stream or the sea and wash away the negative energies they absorbed, recharging and re-energising them.

The other things I love, and still use, are gongs. I have a steel bowl that was made by a Tibetan monk, and when I tap it, it makes the most beautiful sound – absolutely pure, the clearest sound you can imagine. It makes you feel good, calms your breath and raises your vibration. It is very useful for clearing negative energies and shifting residues. It focuses your attention on spirit and is a great way to begin a meditation.

When I started out, all these things fascinated me, and I'm attached to all of them as part of my spiritual journey.

Spirit manifested through writing

LYNDA

Spirit manifests itself in many different ways. Lynda is a spiritual searcher who has the amazing gift of automatic writing, or 'light' writing. This is where her communication with spirit manifests through writing that Lynda appears to produce but which actually is not 'by' her at all. She sits in meditation, holding paper and pen, and the energy vibration flows powerfully into her hands.

Again, this is a wonderful tool. I will be interested to see whether Lynda carries on with automatic writing, or whether, like me, she gets beyond where she needs a skill like this as an intermediary between her and spirit.

She has filled more than 75 exercise books with this writing. She showed me one of her books and it was absolutely amazing and very beautiful – page after page filled with writing in many different handwriting styles and languages. She has no doubt that this experience is given to her by a force outside of herself.

Lynda first became aware of spirit in 1994 when an aunt who had medically 'died' returned to life with some amazing gifts. An illiterate woman, she was able to speak long extracts from books, and she had visions that told her exactly what was wrong with people. She told Lynda, 'You have an amazing spiritual connection, just like I have.'

Lynda had always known that she had a particular kind of sensitivity; for instance, being able to walk into a room and tell whether things were right. She was very sensitive to residue – the things that have happened previously in a place.

She began meditating, and through that opened herself up to spirit and the gift she had been born with: the voice of spirit flows through her hands, or into her being as a form of knowing.

'I spent hours in meditation. I knew there was something there, I knew it existed. It began flowing really quite powerfully, more and more in the last few years. The energy vibration flowed powerfully into my hands and I began writing very, very fast. I know I cannot write that fast myself. It's a power that is beyond my own physical capabilities.

'Some people call it light writing, some people call it channelling. I can't give it a name. I just know it's such a positive vibration and it's given with the purest form of love imaginable. I feel that. There's no negativity, there's nothing there that's bad. It feels like a blessing. I'm at peace when I'm writing. I'm in the zone between the worlds, yet very conscious of what's going on around me.

'When I'm writing it's often in a foreign language first, and then there's the English translation underneath it. When I read it over, I can almost guarantee that what is written in that day I will see or feel, or some circumstance will come which is almost identical to what's written there. It's almost like a daily message for me.'

Describing the physical feeling of energy she receives, she says it's like when you rub your hands together and then hold them, palm to palm without actually touching. The energy is warm and strong yet gentle and exciting.

Her great desire is to help others with her gift, and in fact she's already starting to do this. 'I can run my hands over someone's body and know exactly where the ailments are. If someone comes to me with a problem, I sit quietly and let the writing flow and I share that. Sometimes I'll be with someone and they might be voicing a concern about a family member, for instance, and I can feel the answers in my head. It might come out, and I'll say, "Did I say that? That wasn't me!"'

Lynda is a professional photographer and often sees orbs in her photos. Orbs are those little circular lights that appear in some photos. Sometimes they can be quite detailed images of spirit. There is no technical explanation for them. They are spirit light – visual proof that our loved ones in spirit are there with us. Lynda says she loves seeing them in photos.

'It's lovely knowing we're not alone, and that it's not just mankind on earth. It gives me this knowing: that wherever we go and whatever we do, we're guided, and that's so exciting.'

The Listening Meditation

I ask spirit for protection and for the faith to trust in the messages I receive from spirit.

This is a lovely meditation – one of my favourites. You just put on some cool, spiritual music or sounds and let your vibrational energy rise!

When we tune in to the sounds around us and really bring them to the fore, rather than pushing them to the back of our consciousness, we are activating our senses. Our own frequency becomes heightened, our awareness is alerted, pinged into life, and we become much more tuned in to spirit energy.

Spiritual music can be incredibly helpful when we're meditating. As well as drowning out background noises, it also inspires us, opening up the pure, spiritual sensation in our mind and body. In meditation we listen in a different way from how we usually do: we listen with our ears and our bodies, but also our hearts. We follow the music in a way we don't usually

– and we let it carry us into a new, intense spiritual energy. Interestingly, a lot of spiritual music designed to aid meditation uses wind instruments; so, just as we're focusing on our breath, so the music is inspiring us with breath, manifesting as beautiful music.

Before you do your basic preparation, you need to get yourself organised. Choose a CD, or have a look on the internet. There is an enormous amount of free, legally downloadable spiritual music available from all over the world. Listen around and find something that really speaks to you.

My personal top five are these. First, Sacred Spirit's album of the same name. There's a track on there called 'Yeha Noah', and when I first heard it I had a powerful vision of a Native American priest in full regalia, standing on a hill singing to the Creator. Second: Deva Premal's album *The Essence.* Third, I love listening to the sound of the Maori flute, the koauau. Fourth: a CD of Aboriginal chants using the didgeridoo. Fifth: anything to do with chants, such as Buddhist chants. I also love to listen to natural sounds on CD, like dolphins, whales or birdsong. You see, it doesn't have to be music. When I first found a CD of dolphin song I thought, 'Dolphins, choice, I'll meditate to that.' Three or four meditations later it was almost as if they were talking to me. My awareness was so high, my vibration was so up there, I absolutely felt that I had entered the spirit realm. Anything that lifts you high and low is great for meditating. What I mean by that is that it heightens you, and then it mellows out to find a sense of stillness, and then it lifts you up again on a fascinating journey.

Before you start your meditation, you could also try stimulating your other senses to create a really beautiful environment. Light some incense, light a candle, put on your CD and give yourself permission to just exist inside the music.

Do your prayer, and your calming breathing. Focus on your body: do a quick scan, releasing tension, breathing into any aches you might be experiencing. Bring your attention gently to the music. As you breathe in, feel the space inside your head expanding and filling with the music; as you exhale, sink further into the musical energy. Follow the music. Just follow it. If you find your attention has drifted, just gently bring it back to the music.

This is a very opening, very energising meditation, and you will feel wonderful afterwards. When you're ready to stop, wait for the end of the song and allow yourself to register the feeling of the silence that comes. Be aware of your breath, of your body. Give your prayer of thanks for having been opened to spirit in this way. Open your eyes.

Ludwig van Beethoven, one of the most important musical composers of all time, said, 'Music is the mediator between the spiritual and the sensual life.' He knew what he was talking about. When we put music into our spiritual practice, we definitely feel ourselves drawing closer to spirit.

STEP SEVEN

Acceptance

God, grant us the...
Serenity to accept things we cannot change,
Courage to change the things we can, and the
Wisdom to know the difference
Patience for the things that take time
Appreciation for all that we have, and
Tolerance for those with different struggles
Freedom to live beyond the limitations of our past
 ways, the
Ability to feel your love for us and our love for
 each other and the
Strength to get up and try again even when we
 feel it is hopeless.

–Reinhold Niebuhr, theologian

Cancer was the catalyst for Josie's interest in spirituality. 'People often say that you learn the most in your darkest hours and that was certainly true for me,' she says.

Diagnosed with thyroid cancer at just 24, she was told she had only six months to live. From that traumatic moment, she says, 'Everything was up for negotiation. My spiritual journey happened as a consequence of my cancer experience. Before that I wasn't really a spiritual person – moderately religious, but definitely not spiritual. I started questioning everything I'd ever been taught. I'd been taught that bad things don't happen to good people, so I thought, if there's a God, why would he do this to me? I asked lots of questions, and found that the answers did not align with my experience up till then.'

Her experience gave her a passionate interest in the subject of fear, and how it plays out in everyday life. That in turn led her into what has become her new career, as a life coach. She's now one of Australia's top life coaches and a really cool woman. I met her when she came along to one of my workshops.

'When I talk to cancer patients, it's almost as if we have our own language,' she says. 'When you're going through it, it doesn't feel like courage. It doesn't feel like bravery. It's just a choice that you're making to take charge of the experience.

'There are two types of cancer patients. There are the ones that think they can be cured. They're not kidding themselves. They've just got this peace within them, that it'll be what it'll be, and they consciously try to have a more positive experience of the journey, regardless of the outcome. And there are those that believe the prognosis and seem to give in, and give up their life. It's really sad, but it's their choice to determine how their experience of cancer impacts them.

'I would never abandon hope of conquering disease, as it is my firm belief that "healing" is possible in any situation. However, it is not completely cynical to say that while any disease is curable, some patients are not.'

She believes that fear is behind many illnesses. 'I think we make our bodies ill,' she says. 'There's purpose and meaning in every experience.'

As Josie acknowledges, there are so many fears that hold us in place: fear of failure, of success, of being alone or abandoned, of rejection, of expressing our true feelings, of intimacy. And of course, the big one – fear of death, which she describes as 'paralysing'.

Her first cancer scare made her realise how afraid she was of dying, and it was only after a lot of seeking and questioning that she found peace within herself – acceptance, in a word, and a renewed sense of the miracle of life. One of her favourite sayings became, 'Life is not measured by the number of breaths we take, but by the moments that take our breath away.'

She is a great advocate of meditation and prayer.

'These kinds of activities open a direct link between yourself and the spiritual realm. Meditation and prayer can bring you peace, clarity, joy and connection. It can bring you closer to your Creator and can assist in experiencing a perfectly balanced state between your mental, physical, emotional and spiritual self,' she says.

'Fear is the glue that keeps you in place; it keeps you from moving ahead and keeps you from realising your dreams,' she explains. 'Fear is subtle and covert and uses guerrilla tactics to sabotage your efforts to succeed. But more importantly, it has a deleterious effect on your physical body, and I certainly learnt that the hard way!

'Fear is the progenitor of many afflictions, from which you can also experience anxiety, panic, resentment, anger and rage. All of these symptoms produce stress and I strongly believe that stress is the leading cause of, or at least a significant contributor to, a myriad of diseases. Most of us don't want to admit to ourselves, much less to others, that we have fears. However, admission and awareness go hand-in-hand. Awareness is the first step towards change and it is also the springboard to greatness.'

Josie believes it's important to keep fear in perspective, and she has some great ideas for managing it in your life. First, she says, it's important to realise that fear is a gift: 'It's a universal emotion that helps us set boundaries around dangerous people and situations that can cause us harm. It's a tool in our toolbox of self-awareness, and it gives us information that it's important to acknowledge, for the sake of our mental and physical health. We can see it as an aid for self-development.'

Incredibly, about 18 years after her first cancer experience, Josie was hit again, this time with a brain tumour. In the course of her illnesses, surgery and treatment, she has had three experiences of dying.

'The first time I died, I had the experience of floating above my body and looking down. It was so serene, it was very peaceful, it was white, it was beautiful, and I heard a voice, a male voice that very strongly said to me, "It's not your time yet." And I felt myself go straight back into my body at light speed.

'The second time it happened, that same voice said, "It's not your time yet." The voice was assertive, and it wasn't frightening, but it was like, "You do as you're told", kind of thing. There was no fear.

'But this time, when I had the brain tumour, it was different. I was told that I would have to make a choice, and whatever choice I made it would be okay and I would be accepted and loved, no matter what. I didn't have to choose to stay, I didn't have to choose to be here, and I knew that I would have a major responsibility to follow through in my calling here if I chose to stay.'

Josie came to my workshop because of her active curiosity about spirit. I was interested to note that, while she is clearly a very spiritual person, not everything about the workshop suited her. She struggled with the first exercise – where I pair people up with a partner they've never met before, and they try to open themselves to spirit in order to discover things about the other person.

Josie was open about the fact that she was not getting any message about her partner – that she wasn't seeing or hearing anything. 'I sense spirit and I intuit them, not see or hear,' she says.

She's very clear, though, that the matter of communicating with spirit is quite different to using one's imagination. 'You can see things that are not immediately in front of you, but you're talking about a space that's beyond the conscious reality,' she says. 'Imagination is something else entirely. I think imagination is a very powerful tool for manifesting what you want in your life and it can also be a very crippling tool if you're focusing and manifesting the very things that you don't want. It can be extremely powerful.'

However, at the end of the workshop, when we did the exercise of reading a partner using an angel card as a tool, it suited her much better. 'All of a sudden I felt so much more confident to be able to trust my intuitive sense,' she says.

I think this is a really important point: we are all gifted in different ways, with different strengths and abilities. It's important to find a form of spiritual expression that you're comfortable with, and that is meaningful to you. Also, we must be patient and compassionate in our attitude to our own spiritual growth. It doesn't all happen at once.

Josie says, 'I feel like I'm an awakening being. I'm open to growth and learning, and spirituality becoming a central piece of my whole reality.'

I think that's inspirational. She went on to say that, on reflection, she wondered whether her inability to see or hear spirit in that first exercise was because she 'didn't really slow down enough to create space to allow messages to come in. In that space I was forcing it. It happens when it's meant to happen, not when you want it to happen.'

That's another great learning – you see, when we go away and reflect on our experiences, there is always something to take on board.

For Josie, that learning about creating space and time for spirit is especially poignant, as it relates closely to the lessons she's taken from each of her illnesses.

'The message the first time was to stop living a life of duty and obligation, speak up, and create your own powerful reality. I found my voice through that experience. I actually said no for the first time to a lot of people and bravely faced a whole new journey.

'The second one hit me out of the blue and when I felt into it, the message was: you live your life at such a crazy pace, and we've been wanting you to slow down and stop, and if you're not going to do it, here's the deal! You know, you get a little tap to take note, then if you don't get it or you're not listening you get a knock, and if you still don't get it, there's a big whack which you can no longer ignore!'

Listen to spirit, in other words. It has so much to teach us about how to live our lives. When we listen to spirit, when we make time to connect to spirit with love, our lives become harmonious and meaningful, and we keep our feet and our hearts on the right path. Pay attention, listen to the messages of your body, and listen to the messages of your heart.

Josie reminded me of this quote from William Jennings Bryan: 'Destiny is not a matter of chance, it is a matter of choice; it is not a thing to be waited for, it is a thing to be achieved.'

First steps along the way

From Josie's story, we can see how overcoming fear and even rage and adopting instead an attitude of acceptance and faith can completely transform our experiences, even of something as horrendous as two bouts of cancer. Here we can clearly see how acceptance opened Josie up to come closer to spirit, whereas her fear would have left her stumbling around in the dark.

An important point here is that acceptance is not passive. It is very, very active. It is not rolling over and giving up; it is grasping your challenges, looking them in the eye, acknowledging them, and dealing with them in an active, positive way. Acceptance is the first step along the way.

Not everyone is able to achieve acceptance. For some people, the fear is just too great, and they bravely try and deal with their experience by denial – refusing to talk about what's happening to them, or to face up to either the disease, or their own death, if that is what is coming. This is tragic, and brings so much extra pain, not only for the person who is ill, but for the people around them as well. Their family and friends see their psychological distress and are powerless to do anything to help – in fact, they are often not allowed to do anything to help, as the person with the illness closes down all offers of emotional support.

In these cases, the comfort offered to the living person through connection with their loved one in spirit is absolutely incredible. To see someone's anguish fall away, and their grief move into a more positive stage is one of the best things in the world for me. Spirit can teach us so much about how to live. It validates us, and cloaks our experiences – even our saddest ones – with love and hope.

People come to my shows for many reasons, but the two main ones are that they need closure – the chance to say goodbye to someone who, for some reason, was not able to say goodbye – and because the person who passed was in so much pain that the person living cannot stop worrying about them.

Breaking free of pain and fear

HAYLEY

Hayley came to a show hoping for a message from her best friend Sharon, who had passed three months earlier of breast cancer, aged just 43.

I had been reading for her friend sitting next to her when I suddenly got an overwhelming sense of a new spirit presence. 'I'm getting an impression of Sh,' I said. 'This is a friend who has passed. Who is Sharon?'

'Oh my God!' Hayley folded her arms across her chest in shock at hearing her friend's name.

'I said "friend",' I carried on, 'but Sharon is letting me know that this was much more – more like sisters.'

This was accurate. Sharon and Hayley and a third woman, Kelly, had been best friends since they were teenagers. Sharon was 36 when she first got sick, and from that day on she had lived in terrible fear and grief – especially because she was so afraid of leaving her young daughter behind. (Sharon's daughter was just 14 when her mother died.)

Sharon never came to terms with her illness, refusing to let doctors even talk to her about what was likely to happen, and never letting even her closest friends talk to her about dying. While her family and friends respected her wishes, understanding that she knew no other way of coping with the horror, this also made it very difficult for them to address their own feelings about what was happening. Sharon's illness, so dominant in their lives, was nevertheless a taboo subject. 'Sharon just closed us down,' Hayley says.

While Sharon was in hospital receiving chemotherapy, the friends planned a Thelma and Louise-type trip through America in a Mustang convertible. Once Sharon was out of hospital, they actually did it, driving from LA to Vegas, doing the Grand Canyon – 'all the things we'd dreamed about', as Hayley says. 'I was just so desperate for her to let herself go and enjoy the moment.'

But Sharon never really could – although on the surface she was often still the same person, telling rude jokes about the doctors with Hayley and Kelly, and laughing at the most inappropriate things. Her cancer came back with a vengeance, moving into her lungs, making her sicker and sicker.

During the reading, Sharon told me that she and Hayley had matching tattoos, and she thanked her friend for her love. She told me how, just four days before she died, Hayley had taken her out in her wheelchair with her oxygen bottle to the shopping mall where they'd had a coffee and looked around the shops, just like old times. 'She was so stubborn and so determined,' Hayley says.

'Who's Lisa?' I asked Hayley. 'She says she's with Lisa.'

'That's Kelly's sister,' Hayley replied. 'She passed away years ago.'

'Now she's showing me Freddie Mercury!' I said. 'You know in that song, "I Want to Break Free", where he's dancing around with the vacuum cleaner? That's what she's showing me. She wants you to know that she's no longer in physical pain. She's broken free. Even though it's so sad, she wants you to know that she's living her life over there. She says she wished she'd talked more. She's so sorry. She was scared. Actually, she says she was "petrified". Phew,' I said, suddenly understanding what Hayley had been through. 'She can be difficult, man!'

'Yes,' Hayley agreed, laughing. 'She could be really stroppy.'

The next message to come through was an image of Hayley's little son, and a strong impression of a dog. 'Does he want a dog?' I asked her.

'He asks every day!' she said. 'But I don't want a dog...' So that was a way in which Sharon could show her that she was still there in her life, aware of what was going on.

'I'm so happy that she's okay and happy,' Hayley told me later. 'I really feel as if a huge weight has lifted off me. Sharon's struggle, her passing – it was just awful, and to have this lovely message, well, that's what I'll now focus on rather than that awful ending. When I think about her now, free and whole, it's without all my worries, stress and anxieties. I am on cloud nine!'

A chance to move on

In the afterlife, we get the chance to look at our experiences, accept them for what they were, understand them as best as possible and move on. The ones who have passed are usually better at accepting than the ones left behind.

As we know, spirit continues to care about us and to watch over us – but not 24/7. We're old enough and big enough to look after ourselves. People who, in the physical world, become obsessed and think that their loved ones in spirit are continuously watching them are often a bit deluded. The fact is, they haven't let go themselves; they haven't accepted that their loved one is actually gone.

I had an experience with a woman whose son had been killed by a drunk driver. Her son had been a really amazing young guy – full of beans, everybody loved him, and she was really struggling to come to terms with losing him.

I did a reading for her, and her son came through. It was lovely, a very satisfying reading, and at the end I told her, 'Oh, he's just stepped away from me, he's stepped back and he just leaves his love with you.' This is what happens, because as we know, it takes an enormous effort for spirit to come and talk to us in this way and they can't usually stay long. But she couldn't let him go. She started talking, asking question after question, trying to hold on to him.

'Darling,' I told her, 'you've got to understand, the spirit comes through so they can connect with you. Whether it's just two seconds or twenty minutes, it's still a connection and it's a blessing. But now you're trying to hold on to him. Can you not let him be at peace with where he's at? Because he can't sustain being here, he's tired and you're tired. You need to be able to step back and understand that there will be a time when you can reunite with him, but it's not now. You can meditate on that, you can pray for him, and you'll connect with him. But you can't hold him here, you've got to stop holding on.'

'Oh,' she asked, 'am I hurting him?'

'No, but you're hurting yourself and he doesn't like that.'

We all deal with grief in our own way, but sometimes people need to be told, 'Look, he's not coming home in the way that you want him to.' Some people find that very hard to accept.

The nature of things

Here's a story about acceptance. A frog was on his way home to his family when he came to a stream that was too swollen for him to cross. He looked at his family on the other side and he wondered how he was going to get home. A crocodile came along and said, 'Hey, I'll take you over. Hop on my snout, I'll take you across.'

'But you'll eat me,' said the frog.

'No, no, no,' the crocodile insisted. 'I won't eat you. I'll take you across.'

So, the frog jumped on the crocodile's snout, and off they went. But when they were nearly at the other shore, the crocodile tossed the frog into the air and caught him in its mouth.

'You gave me your word!' cried the frog. 'Why are you eating me?'

And the crocodile said, 'It's just my nature.'

Some people cling to the ones they love, even when not letting go means they are pulling everything down around them. Instead, they need to learn what life is. It's just nature being nature, and we need to accept that people do pass on. It's okay to talk to your family that have passed, to remember them, to acknowledge them and, obviously, to love them. But some people take this too far and behave almost as if the other person is still living. This drains the life out of both themselves and people around them.

They need to accept: people pass on. We still love them, and they still love us. But we are no longer in the same realm. They are not coming back. It is our job now to get on and live our own life as best we can. That is the best tribute we can give our loved ones who are now in spirit – and that is always what they want for us.

There's no room for resentment and spirit to co-exist. When you're feeling resentful and clingy, spirit gets pushed aside. When we find acceptance, we open up once again to all the possibilities of spirit. We feel spirit move once again in our hearts and, ironically, we are more connected to our loved ones than when we were clinging to them so relentlessly.

In the end, of course, the only person who can make these changes is you. I know – I always say that! But it is true and that is a wonderful thing, is it not, that we have within ourselves the power to transform our lives. When we set off down that path – and we take the first step on the journey when we decide to embrace acceptance – we will be supported by spirit, and the love of our loved ones who have passed. They only want the best for us. They want us to be happy and to enjoy our lives. It is only when we accept their passing that they themselves can truly find peace. So, acceptance is a gift both for us, and for our loved ones in spirit.

Acceptance leads to understanding, to faith, to an increased belief in the love that is spirit. We can't control life – what happens, happens. It is just in the nature of things. We are not the Creator; we are the Creator's children, experiencing this wonderful playground that is life. I have faith, knowing that the Creator for me is all loving and all understanding, and that even in my darkest hour, spirit will guide me and protect me.

Sometimes we struggle to accept

I have been given a wonderful gift by spirit – the gift of communicating with people who have passed; the gift of seeing into the past and future. There have been times in my life when I have tried to push this gift away, unable to accept it. When I did accept it, I realised that I had been given this gift in order to help people, and this I do: I am a medium between the living and the dead, bringing their messages of love, in order to help people get over their grief and carry on living in a positive way.

But sometimes this work is extremely hard. To bring these messages forward for people is not easy. The way spirit communicates with me is by letting me actually experience their earthly experiences, so that I can understand and translate it into a message of words to pass on to the living.

Often this is overwhelming. It can be overwhelming in a good way – such as when I actually feel the love that is between people. But it can also be overwhelmingly hard, as when a spirit brings forth a lot of darkness to show me how they were abused. In the work I did on *Sensing Murder,* it was often incredibly hard to handle, as I not only saw things that were completely horrific, but also felt the experiences of those people who were murdered.

It's scary, I can tell you. No one could see these things and not have it affect their mind. It would often take me weeks to recover from those readings, and I was sometimes completely traumatised. Yet, I have to accept it. I can't push it away. I have this gift, and that means I must be strong enough to bear it. It's been given to me for a purpose and so therefore I must use it.

So, acceptance for me is a particularly poignant issue – to accept my gift and all the things it brings, while always reminding myself that I don't own any of these experiences, good or bad. If I tried to own them, I would create a prison for myself. I have to experience these things, accept them, and let them go. That's something I can only do within myself by being in solitude and using prayer and meditation – in other words, through God or spirit, which helps and strengthens me. It's like the prayer says, 'Give me the serenity to accept the things I cannot change, courage to change the things I can, and the wisdom to know the difference.'

When they can't accept they've died

Even after all the things I've seen, I am still sometimes shocked by things I see in spirit. Imagine how I felt during a show one night when, in the middle of a nice reading with a family whose father had come through in spirit, I looked towards the back of the hall and there was a body hanging from the ceiling –

in spirit, of course! He swung there for just a few seconds, and then he was gone.

What happened was this: when people commit suicide, they go into what I call a limbo space. They usually kill themselves when they're in a dark, negative space, and quite often there are drugs or alcohol involved.

Suicide where drugs are involved interferes with the path you chose with the Creator – your true path in life. Drugs confuse the soul. It is common, at the moment of death, for the soul to step away from the body and be struck by the terrible recognition of what they've just done – and that there's no going back. I've often had spirit say to me, 'I was on P [methamphetamine]. If I was straight I wouldn't have done it.'

Their realisation brings shame, guilt and resentment. They cannot accept that they've died. They often realise the damage they've done to the people they love.

These people are alienated from love – from self-love, and from forgiveness, and they're lost and confused and unable to move on spiritually.

The physical manifestation in which they come through is often with the body language of guilt and shame – their heads are down, their shoulders are slumped, and they won't look me in the eyes. I've learned that if a spirit won't look at me directly, it's often because they were a suicide case. They often want to ask for forgiveness. They need to learn to love themselves, and to find their way into the light.

Now, before I open any reading or show, I always bless the place I am working in, and ask for the white light to open up above us.

One of the people in the audience that night was a friend of this man and he was unable to stop thinking about the man who had hanged himself. He came to the show hoping to make a connection. The fact that he'd come to the show was all that was needed for his friend to come through, out of limbo and into the white light that we'd created for the show – it's like a moth to the flame. This is soul rescue.

'So,' I told his friend, 'you've done a good thing by coming here tonight. Your friend was lost, but he's now going to cross through properly.'

Often, when there's a suicide involved, the spirit will be too shy to come up the front to talk to me. I'll get the sensation that spirit is there and wants my attention, and then I'll see a guy standing in the very back of the theatre with a rope in his hand. I'll think, oh, okay, he's committed suicide; he's too scared to come up to talk to me right up the front. So, I'll say to him in my mind, 'Hey mate, how can I help?'

'Here to see my sister, mate.'

'Oh, well, where is she?'

'Oh, I'm pretty shy.'

I'll be having this conversation all by myself, just in my head, in a matter of seconds. And I'll say, 'Come on then, show me.'

He'll walk down the aisle, going in behind people, and he'll become illuminated as he gets closer to the person he needs to speak to. These situations are often very hard because the person in spirit just wants to come back. And of course he can't. So I need to help him acknowledge and accept that he's passed, and help him go into the white light. It's very sad, and of course I feel that sadness right through my body.

They're not my feelings

The feelings associated with suicide, though, are different to the feelings associated with people who have done serious harm to others during their lifetime. For example, when someone comes to me for a reading and there's been child molestation in the family history, I am instantly swept with a feeling that is so dark I have to work very hard afterwards to let it go. I tell myself it's not my feeling, I don't own it, I didn't do it. I just have to accept that I am given these feelings to experience so that I can help.

Those are the sorts of things I try not to think about too often.

One time a mother and her three daughters came for a family reading. Her husband – their dad – had passed over. He came through, and initially portrayed himself as a really nice person in spirit. He acknowledged the girls, and had some nice messages for them, and so on. However, I found as I was doing the reading that I was unable to look at one of the girls, and so my alarm bells started ringing.

I stopped the flow of conversation, and asked the women to wait for a minute, and I went deeper into my communication with this guy – into what we call a deeper trance state.

I asked him, 'What's the story? Why do I feel uncomfortable when I try to look at your daughter?' Well, he turned away from me. In spirit, he turned his back on me, and I knew straight away. I thought, 'Oh strewth, do I have to go there?' And my guides, my angels, were going, 'Yeah, got to go there.' I mean, that's pretty serious. When spirits come through and drop their heads, they're guilty of something and feel ashamed and sorry, and they're really acknowledging that they've hurt people. But when they turn their back on me, it means there is not only serious trouble in their background, but they are still in denial about the damage they've done. In other words, there is no acceptance.

I forced myself to look at the daughter and asked, 'Dad hurt you, didn't he?'

She started to shake. I looked across the room and I could see that the two other girls knew, but the mother had no idea.

The man in spirit got angry with me. 'Don't go there, don't go there,' he screamed at me.

I said to the daughter, 'Look, we need to get this out so we can release it. Your dad has turned his back on me and that's how I know there has been an experience with you and him.' I could tell that, while the other girls had also had a bad experience with their father, things had gone much further with this one. 'You were the youngest,' I acknowledged, 'so he was able to manipulate you a bit more. And I think it's time to tell Mum.'

She told her mother, and the other girls backed her up and told about their own experiences, but their mother was saying, 'I can't believe it, I can't believe it.' And yet it became apparent that she had kind of known – but she had not wanted to know. It was a terrible mess.

Things like this are excruciatingly painful, even just to talk about, because it's such a mixed bag of emotion and tragedy.

The mother was saying, 'I'll not have this, I'll not have this talk.'

'Well,' I told her, 'we're going to, we have to, and I'm here to be able to bring this up because it's important for your daughter.'

I sat back and let them talk, and eventually the mum lost the battle, shall we say, of denial. She slumped her head and burst into tears. 'I didn't know how to protect you, and I was frightened of him. He'd done this to me, he'd done that to me. Even though I loved him and all his good points, there was a dark side that nobody really ever saw.'

Someone once told me, 'You'll never heal anyone with your words.' But that's so wrong, because of course you can heal with words. Words set everything free. There is nothing worse than a secret – and it's pointless trying to hide the truth because it will always come out.

Once they were able to talk about these things among themselves, the four women could begin to come to terms with it, accept what had happened and so move on. They had, in effect, rescued their family.

I then asked if I could continue talking to the father for a bit, so that we could try and make peace. The women weren't too impressed with that idea, but I insisted that it was important. It turned out that the father himself had experienced sexual molestation when he was a kid, and so here we have an example of someone who was unable to break the cycle in his own life. During the reading, he began to acknowledge the hurt he'd caused, and he apologised to his family, which was very moving. In that case, the family was unable to accept the apology at that time, which is understandable. I believe that once they have had a chance to sit with the situation for a while, they will accept his apology, and that will be a further step along the way for them being able to let go of what happened.

Spirit in shock

Another situation where acceptance can be very hard for the person in spirit is where there's been an accident and the passing was swift and shocking. I did a reading once during a show for the family of a young man who'd been killed in a car accident. He was just 19, and three of his friends were also killed. Now, that's pretty serious stuff.

For me, I can only describe it as an emotional overwhelmingness when the young guy came through and said, 'My mum's out in the audience and my dad's there too, and my brother and my sister, and I just had my nineteenth birthday yesterday.'

I identified the family in the audience and told them, 'Look, I've got this young guy who's telling me he just had his nineteenth birthday yesterday and he was killed in a car accident, and he wants to let you know that he's okay.'

And of course they lost it, because that's what they came for. But then I heard the boy say, 'I want to come home.' And I just felt so sad, because I couldn't change that; nobody can change that. I told his family, 'Hey look, he's saying that he wants to come home, and he knows that he can't, but this is really hard for him because he just wants to reach out and give you all a hug.'

Of course that brought them and their pain to the fore, because they'd also been trying to hold him in this life. So then it became appropriate that I talk to them about acceptance.

'Look,' I said, 'even though he wants to come home and give you a hug, and if he could he would, he accepts that he can't, and you too have to start learning to accept it instead of trying to hold on to him. He's okay because he's with other family members. He's telling you he had a great life, and he is okay and he doesn't like seeing you sad.'

When they hear such a clear message from spirit, it's often easier for the living to begin to accept their loss. Having the contact, knowing that their boy was okay in spirit, was enormously empowering for the healing process for that family. And so their grief began to wane. And that in turn made it easier for the son in spirit to also move on. So, there is a relationship between the pain of the living and the pain of spirit, and they can very much help each other.

Meditation

THE BRIDGE OF LOVE

I ask spirit for protection, and for the patience to understand that I can't run before I walk. I ask for the guidance to accept the things I can't change, to accept the loss of the people I love, but not to lose sight of the power I do have within me to change my world for the better. I ask for guidance to accept that communication with my loved ones in spirit will come, not when I demand it, but when it is the right time.

Now that you're a bit more practised at this meditation gig, we're going to do a really powerful one. Using the power of your own mind, you are going to experience your loved one in spirit, and provide them with an opportunity to meet you in the zone. They will be there, although you might not be ready to see or hear them. But you will feel them.

Do your prayer and get yourself ready with some deep breaths to take you into your spiritual zone. Keep breathing in the way that you now know, and as you become more relaxed, more focused, allow yourself to think of someone who has passed that you're really missing, and who you would like to receive a message from.

Think of their face, the feeling of their physical presence. As the image from your memory floods your conscious mind, allow yourself to really feel this person. Look carefully, noticing things about the way they look, their mannerisms – really bring them to life in your mind. Allow yourself to experience the great love that you have for this person.

Now, think back to a time you enjoyed with this person. Keep breathing! This is a very intense exercise, but gently bring yourself back to your own rhythm, your own breath, as you remember this person that you loved so much. What would you like to say to this person? Make a simple message – that you miss them; that you love them – and as you exhale, transmit that message from yourself to that person. Finish your message with a feeling of finality – like a mental full stop – to indicate that you have finished.

Now you just sit quietly, and you bring your focus gently back to your breathing. Notice whether a replying message comes into your mind. If it does, don't question it. Just calmly register it, and offer another of your own. If you can't feel any sensation of a reply, don't worry. That's absolutely fine. You can send another message anyway, in the same way. Enjoy the feeling of being with this person who is so actively in your mind's eye.

Before you finish this meditation, thank spirit for showing you this person, and for allowing you to experience them so strongly. Ask once again that you can accept that they have passed. Acknowledge your love for them, and accept their love for you.

When we think of them they are there, whether we can detect it with our senses or not.

As you continue doing your work of opening your third eye, and learning how to go deeper into the meditative state, your ability to see, hear and feel spirit will definitely increase.

STEP EIGHT

Listen to spirit

All spiritual disciplines are done with a view to still the mind. The perfectly still mind is universal spirit.

–Swami Ramdas, philosopher and philanthropist

Silence. How often in our daily lives do we ever encounter it? Yet it has been said that God's one and only voice is silence. In silence we can know spirit – truly know, through our own experience, rather than hearing someone else's version.

When we connect to spirit in this way – by creating that opportunity for stillness and silence, and opening ourselves up to spirit through our prayers and meditation – all our usual concerns eventually fall away. At first when we meditate we find it hard as we're not used to sitting so still and being so quiet. Our minds tell us we're being ridiculous, that it won't work, and we're wasting our time. But stay with it. Acknowledge those thoughts and place them aside. Eventually, we begin to move past them.

All the concerns that we typify as being tied to our ego – our feelings about ourselves as we operate in the daily world – cease to preoccupy us and we get the most amazing feeling of losing ourselves as an individual. Instead we become one with the universe – with every creature, every other individual – and at one with the planet and with spirit. It is literally mind-altering. This is one of the great mysteries of the universe, how, by losing our individual ego, we are more fully ourselves; we are at peace and enter into the river of spirit to bathe in love and joy.

In the silence you can listen to spirit, and you can finally hear what your heart sings to you.

Like a love drug

The most important thing that I've ever suggested to you is sit still, do a prayer and please be patient. Don't get peeved off. With all the love in the world I say, just shut up, be still and listen. It works, it does work. Your mind is super powerful. Combine your mind and your heart together ... wicked! You've got some awesome things going on. Working hard on these basic practices, being patient and just keeping going will empower you and enhance your spiritual awareness.

How can you tell when spirit is there, wanting to connect with you? As you develop your spiritual practice you may see, hear or feel them. The initial connection for me brings a feeling that is quite overwhelming, and I feel my body changing, my frequency rising.

A way of describing it is to imagine what it would feel like to jump into a river. Imagine you're at Outward Bound and you just have to do it! You don't know what to expect, how cold the river will be, but you understand that one minute your body will feel one way, and a split second later it will feel very different.

It's the same feeling when a spirit gets close to me. I don't have anything inside my body – it's not a possession – yet my entire body registers the change. I often say it's like going into a petrol station in the middle of summer with the air conditioning, and so it's like walking through a curtain. You go, 'Oh, it's nice and cool now.' It's just the change of dynamics.

Another way of thinking about it is to remember what it's like when you first fall in love with someone and how you're super aware of the other person. You have a heightened sensitivity to this person, and you feel everything's connected, as if you have an amazing bond. You feel as if the world is happy and joyful, and everything else becomes superfluous. Well, multiply that. It's even more intense than that. It's like a love drug!

And that brings me to the next point, because it can be like a love drug, and as we know, love is blind. Sometimes when we make that connection to the spirit world we can become blinded. We get overexcited, and forget to be careful. We forget to look for the difference between the positive and the negative.

People think spiritual connection is a walk in the park, but it takes a lot of energy both from spirit and from the medium. If someone expresses themselves standing there with a rope, can you imagine how hard it is for them to do that? It takes an incredible amount of energy.

And for me, seeing them is like looking down the road when the sun's out and it's hot and you see the shimmer coming up off the tarseal. That energy will sustain for a certain period of time and then disperse.

In short, when we are communicating with spirit, we have to pay attention. We have to watch and listen. Being observant is part of the requirement for talking with people who have passed. I am always aware of everything that is going on around me – the different energies, who is likely to do what, and so on.

In a murder case you have to be acutely observant of everything: people's body movements, their body language, and their eye movements. That's different from reading them – it's just having a knowledge about what things mean; literally, paying attention.

People often ask how we are able to be sure that what we're hearing is really spirit, and not just our own imagination.

When you pay attention to your frequencies, to the feeling of your own body, when you learn to meditate and become one with it all, you'll learn to trust your instincts. You'll learn to trust the voice within and you'll learn not to judge it.

If we do our prayers and our affirmations, in other words create a good grounding, then we relax and stop doubting ourselves because we have left our everyday ego behind and gone into the spirit zone.

When I'm actually communicating with spirit, the best way I can describe what I do is that my own side of the conversation must have a full stop placed at the end of every contribution from me. Once that full stop is put in place, whatever thought comes in from out there is theirs.

Mostly, though, I know the difference because I'm lucky enough to sense the frequency change when someone walks into the room spiritually – and that's the feeling I mentioned before, of a difference that's like plunging your body into a different substance or temperature. However, while it sounds very dramatic, it's actually very subtle.

When you're starting out, it's all about the way you feel, which is why we've been working in this book to help you tune in to yourself and your feelings and thoughts.

If you want to connect with somebody that you love, you have to trust in that love. Feel it, trust the feeling, and your loved one will be with you. All you have to do is close your eyes, remember, and they are there.

This is a little story told to me by a guy I met. He used to work all day in a factory, being really busy managing the machinery and &supervising some of the other guys. It was full on and he certainly had no time to think of his mum who had recently passed.

At the end of the day he got in his car and was like, 'Man, I really wish Mum was here. I could go steal some of her Gingernuts, have a cup of tea and a good old chin-wag about the stress of my day.' But he couldn't go and see his mum because she was over there, so he just thought, 'Well, I wish you were here, Mum.'

And when he had that thought, he could feel the tingling of goosebumps. You know, it's not always your emotions that you're feeling with those sensations; often that tingling is the feeling of spirit. And then he turned the car engine on, thinking, 'Oh, don't be so silly, she's gone, I have to accept it.' The car radio came on and the first song was his mum's favourite song. 'It's so cool when that happens, and I definitely felt close to Mum, and felt her presence with me,' he told me.

So, when we pay attention, we realise that all these little symbols and signs and little crazy, quirky things are spirit's way of communicating – the goosebumps, that feeling that someone's standing behind you even though there seems to be no one there, maybe a little shimmer or a shadow that you just catch out of the corner of your eye. It is their way of attracting our attention, so that they can remind us that they're there, they love us, and they're not far away. There's a very fine line between what we call reality and the spirit realm. They can't be here 24 hours a day; they have lived their life in this physical existence. They're now in the afterlife, but their wairua, their spirit, is there for us. In other words, when we least expect it they will be there.

We understand that when an object moves through space in the physical world it is actually moving through mass. A car that's driving through the air is actually penetrating the energy mass; a ship cuts through the seas. An aeroplane travelling faster than sound generates shock waves, dropping sonic boom along its flight path. So, when spirit enters into our world, there must be an energy reaction between the worlds, and I believe that is the little frisson of energy that we feel when spirit comes close to us.

This is a different matter from residues, which is the reverberation of past activities or people in a space. However, people often notice that, in a home, it will often be in the same spot, again and again, that they notice these little effects – a flicker, a shadow. This is because spirit has identified that spot as safe, like a security blanket, and they'll always come to the same place: 'Right, just keeping an eye on you. All good, eh? Sweet.' They will respect you. They won't get in your face.

Not always what we expect

When spirit comes through, we do have to listen carefully to what they're telling us. So many times in my communications, spirit has been adamant about something, often a name that the person in the audience insists means nothing to them. This is usually because what spirit is telling them is not what they expected to hear.

Funny things often happen in my shows, and it's nearly always because of a combination of this problem of expectation, coupled with the business of interpreting the language of spirit.

A woman came along to a show, hoping for a message from her husband who had recently passed. The first spirit to come forward for her was indeed a man, and I could feel that he had a lot of love for this woman. He was giving me the feeling that his name began with 'F' – in fact, I said, I was pretty certain he was telling me 'Frank'.

'Frank?' the woman said. 'Frank? I don't know any Franks.'

'Are you sure?' I asked her. 'Because he's very insistent, and he's drawing a big love heart for you.'

She carried on denying she knew any Franks, until suddenly a look of pure shock crossed her face. 'Oh!' she gasped. 'Frank! That was my first husband.'

Quite often in my shows people will say 'no' to the names that spirit brings through. I used to worry about this, especially if spirit is very insistent, as it often is. But over the years I have had hundreds of letters from people who have gone away and thought about their reading, and suddenly realised who the message was from. The lesson is, we often expect a certain person to come through for us, but actually the spirit might be someone quite different. We do not always immediately understand what spirit is providing for us, but we can always be sure the message is brought with lots of love. It's just up to us to listen.

One of the funniest things that ever happened in a show involved an elderly woman. She must have been brought along by one of her family members. A man in spirit came through, very insistently wanting me to talk to her. He told me he had died of a heart attack, and his wife – this woman – had tried hard to resuscitate him, doing CPR for quite some time, but he couldn't be brought back. She had blamed herself for his death, and had always wondered if she could have done something different that would have kept him alive. His message to her was, 'It's not your fault. You did everything you could have, but it was my time to go.'

The woman sat up straighter as I was talking to her, delivering her husband's message. She looked mystified and rather cross. 'Eh?' she said. 'Who are you talking to?'

'Your husband,' I told her, patiently. She sniffed in disbelief. 'You can't be talking to him. He's dead!' she said, as the audience exploded in laughter.

The patient fisherman

To connect with spirit is a 50–50 effort. I believe the white light of heaven is just at arm's length – just across the way, just out of sight of us on our earthly plane. I meet them halfway along the path between there and here. It does take an effort, and my effort is this: I have to prepare myself, I have to set a good foundation. Preparation and discipline must be there, and then I ask for protection, and then I ask for a blessing. If it's a show, then the blessing is for the people in the audience. And then I go into the zone, and I just wait – exactly like a patient fisherman waiting for a fish to bite.

During my shows, I often invite everybody to take a quiet moment to imagine their loved ones who have gone before, the ones they want to speak to. I ask people to imagine them, to try and see their faces clearly, to remember the last time they sat together and had a laugh. This is an incredibly powerful exercise, very intense, very focused. It's not unlike the feeling you get in church when everyone is praying. It's very emotional, of course, but also, as they're 'imagining' their people in spirit, the room becomes incredibly busy. When they do that simple exercise, they are actually doing what I do.

People get worried that the spirit isn't really there, that it's all just happening in their own head. But I know that's not the case because I can see the room filling up with spirits. They're standing there, and I can talk to them, and the proof is that they'll tell me things I couldn't possibly know – things that have meaning only to themselves and to the living person sitting in the audience.

For me, it's like when you walk into a crowded party and everyone's talking to you at once because they're all so excited to see you. It can suddenly seem like too much, and then I ask my guides for protection – and it's almost as if a transparent wall comes up around the stage to give me a bit of space.

At the same time that I can see all these spirits – people standing behind their loved ones, dogs and cats running up and down the aisles – I can also hear. It's hard to describe, but it's like a whisper, not unlike the sound of a crowd quietly talking before a show starts.

Sometimes the whispering confuses me. For instance, recently I was halfway through a reading and suddenly I heard something like, 'Did you notice his shoes?' I looked around thinking someone was beside me talking, but it was spirit. I said, 'Hey, did you say something about shoes?' and they went, 'Yeah.' 'Okay, cool as. Can you not do that please, because it can confuse me.'

The confusing thing – and this is incredibly hard to explain in &ordinary, human language – is that spirit don't actually talk. They transmit a vibrational tone, which someone like me picks up and translates into language that I hear. It's like chucking a big tin of spaghetti words into a computer, and having the computer unscramble it all for you in an instant. Except that it's all happening in my head!

Now, here's an interesting point of view on this phenomenon of people thinking about spirit, and spirit filling the room. When people realise this is actually happening, they think that we, the living, are all very powerful and that we can, with our thoughts and prayers, bring spirit to stand beside us. But I kind of think the opposite – that our spirits trigger our thoughts. That is, that they instigate the contact. It is spirit that bring the living to see me, rather than the other way round.

For instance, one older woman was grieving very badly for her husband who had passed. Her adult daughter was spending some time with her, and was browsing around on her mother's computer. She doesn't know how it happened, but she accidentally came across an advertisement for one of my shows. She insists she wasn't looking for any such thing; would never even have thought of it herself. But there it was, and she found herself, without a second thought, buying a ticket then and there. She took her mother along to my show and they got a lovely reading, with the husband coming through with very loving messages that greatly comforted his wife. The daughter, who had never had any contact with spiritualism before this, had a strong feeling of inevitability about the whole thing. I believe it was her father in spirit who engineered the whole thing.

I'll give you another example. You're in a café with your mates but you've kind of switched off and you're thinking about your nan and how much you miss her. You're thinking about how you used to go out for coffee with her. You look across the room and there's an old lady sitting there with permed hair, just like your nan's, and as you watch, she crooks her finger around her cup exactly as your nan used to do. And that sight makes you miss your nan really powerfully, just for that minute.

Is it your memory, then, or is it spirit, your nan, standing behind you saying, 'Hey look, I can show you that I'm still around by giving you a sign'?

I prefer the latter, because I know my own nan shows me when she's round in lots of different ways. Because I'm psychically attuned I get things like, 'I'm here, son, it's all right.' Or, 'Come on Kel!' That's what I'll hear. But then there are times when I actually see her walking through my kitchen when I'm upset, and she'll come and sit with me and she'll say, 'It's okay, boy, we'll get through this, just hang tight.' I know I'm very lucky to have this connection.

Starting out, you just need to make the effort to focus on those people. And then the faith becomes stronger as you go along. Faith is always a huge part of spirituality. Just because you can't see spirits with your physical eyes doesn't mean they're not there.

Some people find the work hard. It's like going to the gym. They start off with good intentions but they don't get there regularly, or they can't be bothered. It's only you as an individual who can actually take you to a higher level. I couldn't do it for you, and nor could your best friend. You've got to do it yourself.

Sorting out the jigsaw puzzle

The language of spirit is not like our own. Spirit communicates, not through spoken words, but through feelings and sensations. Depending on your particular strength, you might tune in to spirit through visions or hearing or feelings. Some people detect spirit presence through smell and taste. Some of us use all these faculties. The main ones for me are feelings and images.

People, especially sceptics, don't think through how difficult it can be to decipher meaning from the communications of spirit. Let me give you an example. In *Sensing Murder,* for instance, spirit doesn't sit down with you and tell you a straight narrative of their life. Not at all. The way I receive what they offer is like a very, very fast filmstrip, filled with images and sensations. From that, I have to decipher what the important, salient points are, that are relevant to this murder investigation.

Because spirit is communicating with image, I might be receiving a very persistent message, and yet not really know what is meant by it. An excellent case in point was Angela Blackmoore who was screaming at me, in spirit, '13–26, 13–26', over and over again. It took me a while to figure that out, but I realised she must have been stabbed 39 times. That turned out to be right, and imagine my horror when I found later on that she'd actually been stabbed 13 times on the hands and forearms, and 26 times on her body. Spirit knows and communicates as best it can.

Spirit communication is often like the pieces of a jigsaw, and it's up to me to fit them together. Sometimes, of course, I just need to ask. When I'm doing readings between family members, the images spirit uses are very important to the experience of that spirit and its living family, but not at all significant to me. I rely on the person living to help me figure out what exactly the spirit is trying to communicate. It can be quite a process, as I am as likely as anyone to draw my own conclusions, to try and guess what they mean.

For instance, in one reading I did for a woman, her grandson, who had died aged five, came through. It was a lovely reading, as her mother also came through for her. Her mother was afraid to come through in spirit, but the little boy helped her – usually in cases like this, the elders come through first to make sure everything is safe for the little one to come.

For some reason I was getting a very strong image of a pohutukawa tree, which sounds straightforward, only I didn't know what it was supposed to mean. I guessed it was referring to a birthday, and I asked if the little boy's birthday was in December, or around Christmas? No. But when I actually told the woman I was seeing a pohutukawa tree, it all fell into place. The family had planted a pohutukawa tree in memory of the little boy, and laid a plaque next to it. The little boy showed me the tree as a symbol to his family so that they would truly know it was him.

I love being able to help people realise that the things they do in memory of their loved ones who have passed are known and &appreciated by the people in spirit.

What's on the menu?

Thankfully, being a chef for a good number of years gave me the gift of mind organisation. Inside my mind now I have what I call a menu, and in it is stored every feeling and experience I've had myself, or observed in others. It incorporates smells, images, metaphors, feelings. The menu has many different categories, just like a restaurant menu does. But instead of 'entrée', 'main', dessert' and so on, mine has 'cancer', 'murder', 'car crash' and so on. It has some beautiful loving categories and some very dark, difficult categories, and it also has a category headed 'laughter'. There is a funny side to readings, and all the spiritual jokes come under 'laughter'. I'll find myself standing on one leg, flapping my arms, and the audience will be in stitches, but it's spirit's way of showing me that he used to be a pilot. Sometimes I'll find myself tapping my feet: it turns out Mum used to be a tap dancer. Spirit loves to make people smile. They want us to be happy. In every category, the multitude of my own experiences and learnings guide me to the meaning of what spirit is telling me.

Everyone who communicates with spirit will have their own special language of communication. This is because spirit communicates with feelings and images, that my brain can only translate according to my own experiences and associations. Thus, when spirit wants me to understand that they carry with them a child who has passed, they cross their arms in front of them in a rocking gesture. This would be understood by most people, but other feelings and images are more individualised to my own life experience.

When someone identifies closely as a church-goer, for instance, I can instantly pick that up because I am so familiar with churches and the feeling they have. Visually, I'll get an image of a necklace with a cross dangling from it, or rosary beads.

It's the same type of sensation as if I said to you, 'Imagine your children at school right now.' You could do that, couldn't you? You could put that picture in your mind's eye of your child in the classroom. You could go into that image and get a lot of detail. Well, it's the same thing, except that I'm seeing something I shouldn't really know.

When spirit comes and tries to show me who they are, they bombard me with images, sensations and feelings. While that's happening, I'm busy checking in with my menu. All I do is ask, 'What is this feeling?'

or, 'Can you open to the page where I am meant to understand this feeling?' My mind will go directly to the part in the menu where I am meant to be.

Sometimes this can take a minute or two, especially if there is something new for me to understand, but generally it all happens in a millisecond. I go deep inside my mind to find the answer to what spirit is trying to show me.

There are some very funny things in my menu, and I'm always adding to it as spirit gives me new experiences to contemplate! One evening at a Soul Food show in the deep south of New Zealand, I was talking to a couple in the back row of the theatre and their friend in spirit kept making me see handcuffs.

I assumed I understood, and began asking them about arrests, police, that sort of thing. They were puzzled – it didn't seem to make any sense. But spirit was very insistent, making me clash and twist the insides of my wrist together. This is often what happens when spirit is trying to make me understand: I'll find my own body making certain gestures, quite spontaneously: tapping my chest (indicates heart issues in the one who passed), holding the little finger of one hand across my chest and drawing it across my breast to indicate breast cancer, placing a finger under an eye and closing the eye to indicate blindness, rubbing my index finger across my teeth to indicate braces, rubbing my tummy in certain ways to indicate bowel cancer, kidney problems or a stomach tumour, and so on.

This time I was a bit confused, so I asked the bloke in spirit to give me a direct answer. 'Fluffy handcuffs,' he finally made me understand. I had to say it to the couple in the audience, 'So what's with the fluffy handcuffs in your wardrobe?'

The girlfriend pointed at her partner and said, 'Ha, that'll teach you for being kinky!'

We all laughed and laughed, 400 people in fits of laughter all because of a set of handcuffs. Clearly the person in spirit was a joker who missed his mates a lot.

A spiritual kick in the backside

Sometimes spirit comes through to give what I call a big, spiritual kick in the backside – that is, a very firm message that the living person might find a bit hard to hear.

A young woman was in the audience one night, and my intuition told me she was feeling defeated by life – as if all the little things had added up to become too much to handle. I was getting the sensation around her of a very messy wardrobe – which doesn't, by the way, mean that I was seeing her actual wardrobe. It's a symbol for me that indicates a person has held on to too much junk – physical, emotional – and can't let things go.

Her grandmother was there for her in spirit. I got chatting to the old lady, and I felt an enormous amount of love and concern coming through.

'Wow,' I said, 'there's so much going on in your head! Your granny is saying, "Stop procrastinating. Get off your high horse and start taking one little step at a time. You can't sit on your hands any more: if you're not happy, it's up to you to do something about it. Rome wasn't built in a day – don't be afraid to take it slow, step by step, rather than being freaked out by the big picture."'

I was getting an image of a deflated children's paddling pool.

'You've got two kids, right?' I asked her. She nodded.

'Well, your granny is telling me you need to relax more with your children. You're missing out on the joy they can bring you. Play more often. Make a few adjustments. When you put in the time and effort, your soul will be fed.'

These were hard words to hear, but the young woman knew they were spoken with love, as she had been very close to her grandmother in life. The old lady left her with a positive message of hope: 'I'm so excited by the next stage forward,' she said.

Visions and what to do with them

When your third eye opens, your mind's eye can fill with powerful visions relating to future events. This can be quite traumatic, and it's important to note that it's not necessarily your own stuff; it can be somebody else's stuff. However, you've been given it, so what should you do with it? You either box it and keep your mouth shut and let it go; or you communicate it. It depends on what is appropriate.

For instance, I was walking with a friend down the street when I suddenly stopped short. My friend asked, 'What's the matter?' And I said, 'Well, see that lady and boy over there?' Across the road there was a woman walking with her nine-year-old son. She was holding his hand, and they looked happy, just cruising along. She said, 'What about it?' And I said, 'He won't make it through the week.'

She said, 'Well, go and tell her. Go and talk to her about it.'

'I can't,' I said. 'It's not my position to. I can see this clearly but I'm not permitted to go over.'

I knew that because, in the instant of seeing what was going to happen, I had asked my spirit guides if I should intervene, and they had forbidden me. At times like that, I have to accept – even though it's really hard – that this event can't be stopped. It is part of the other person's chosen learning to go through that experience.

If my guides had asked me to intervene, I would certainly have crossed the road and approached the woman. And she may have thought I was crackers! But the force wasn't there for me to do that.

And so, the following Friday, the little boy was run over by a truck outside his school. It is very hard to be shown things we are powerless to do anything about.

In readings, it's a different matter. That person has put themselves into the spirit arena, and so there is an inherent permission given that visions will be passed on. The time is right.

In those settings, I believe the vision comes to me because the person has a need to talk about an important issue. My vision will bring their issue out into the open so that they no longer feel isolated and depressed.

If I get a vision and I'm not in a formal reading, I'll do a nice walking prayer, such as, 'Please guys, just protect me, I know that you're there, I'm willing to help if needs be. If you give me permission, I'll go for it and I'll throw the message with confidence.' Then you can say what you need to say.

If I'm just out and about, say in the supermarket, and I receive a vision, my rule of thumb is that I would never disrespect the person by going up to them and saying, 'Hey, I've got your dad here, he wants to say goodbye, he was killed in a car accident.' They haven't given me their permission to read for them, and although their family might be coming through, it's not my place. For all I know, they might be ideologically opposed to spiritualism. If someone has not given you permission, do not get up in their face if you see things for them.

But sometimes the visions are just there to help you learn – to help you to trust what spirit is giving you. You may not need to pass the message on.

When I started out it was all about learning from the experience. 'Okay, I'm getting stuff, am I meant to say anything?' 'No, just learn from it. When the time's right, speak.' I'm still learning! Sometimes I get a vision and its meaning will not be clear. It will be a symbol of something – a metaphor, not meant to be taken literally. In those cases, I need to sit with it in meditation, and actually ask, 'What do I need to take from this?'

However, sometimes it's all too literal. A woman at one of my workshops had a powerful dream of planes crashing into a building, and in her dream she was standing by a telephone booth watching it. She woke up and was so upset she couldn't get back to sleep, so she went and turned on the television ... and watched the horror of 9/11 and the suicide plane attacks on New York's Twin Towers unfold before her.

In my opinion, she had astral travelled. I believe that because she knew exactly where she was in relation to what was going on.

The day before that happened, I was seeing undercarriages of planes, flames, and all I could hear, over and over again, was 'I walk through the valley of the shadow of death'. When George Bush finally got off his chuff and spoke, it was the first thing he said, reciting that Psalm. I just about fell over.

In all of this, where we're trying to get to spiritually is that, when we see things in our visions, we should not be in fear of them. The vision is meant to be there; it just is. We ask ourselves, 'Why?' when we may just as well ask ourselves, 'Why not?'

Meditation

THE SOUND OF SILENCE

I ask spirit for protection and guidance as I begin my journey inwards. I ask for guidance as I explore my relationship with the world around me, and I ask for patience as I attempt to listen to what silence has to tell me.

Okay, so it's pretty hard in this crazy world of ours to find true silence – although if you ever can, it's awesome. If you're in the bush, and you just sit absolutely still, you can feel the universe expanding in all directions, and you eventually really do feel that you're opening yourself up and becoming one with it. Absolute silence is as substantial as a solid object, and it's limitless and boundless.

I love to go diving, and I love the sensation of silence I get when I'm underwater. Of course, it's not really silent at all. The ocean crackles and roars, and yet I experience it like a silence. I'll go right down to about 85 feet and just hang out, enjoying the feeling.

A friend who spent time in the Antarctic told me that once, when he was sitting alone, well away from anyone else, he was contemplating the incredible landscape when he became aware of a persistent little noise. He couldn't figure out what it was for a while, but eventually he realised: it was the sound of his blood moving through his ears! Imagine being in such silence that you could hear that!

Mostly, though, when you go looking for silence you just have to take what you can get, and that's fine for our purposes here. What we're really exploring is the silence within ourselves.

Timing is an important factor with this meditation. Personally, I have always loved to meditate very early in the morning. The quality of the environment is very different at that time. The absence of activity either inside your home, or out in the community, means that your own energy is very clear to you; you are super conscious of yourself.

The world sleeps around you and, of course, you feel the world awakening, the birds starting to sing, and human noise starting to penetrate once again. This morning energy is very potent. It is very energising in a spiritual sense.

Do your preparation, and once you've reached your nice, relaxed, calm inward feeling, slowly extend your consciousness outwards into the world around you.

Become aware of the stillness, and the energy that resides in that stillness. It's an energy of peace and quietness.

Become aware of the little noises – perhaps distant cars, or a dog barking, or simply the little noises of your house. (If you can do this meditation outside, all the better, as you will be even more attuned to the energy of the day beginning to grow out of the silence.)

Hear those noises but don't dwell on them. Let your thoughts, your consciousness, return to the stillness that lies between these sounds. Understand that there is always this stillness there, in between the noises of everyday. In that stillness, you touch spirit.

You can do this as long as you want, practising the sensation of stillness within yourself, noticing and letting go the little sounds around you.

When you are ready to finish this meditation, thank spirit for allowing you to experience the energy of silence.

STEP NINE

Love

> Every human thought, and every human action, is based in either love or fear. There is no other human motivation, and all other ideas are but derivatives of these two.
>
> *–Neale Donald Walsch, modern-day spiritual messenger*

The most important thing is love. It's what binds us together in this world and the next; it creates the pathway between the worlds. With love, all our petty differences can be seen for what they are.

Love is the key to everything. I think the physical world becomes too analytical about everything. You know, when I get up at two o'clock in the morning and my baby daughter is crying and I pick her up, I just love her, and that love soothes her. Does that make sense to you?

No matter how tough a time someone has during this earthly life, no matter how relieved they might be to find themselves in the heavens, it's love that will bring them back to see us.

Love really is the bond that does not die. It never ceases to amaze me, the importance of these connections between people – the love we have for our parents even when we're getting old ourselves; the love we have for our children which never lessens in intensity, even after we've passed on; the way we keep alive the memory of our partner, even when they've gone years before. Humans really do have the most extraordinary capacity for love. It's a fantastic human quality.

I've seen this happen so often in my readings: there'll be someone in the audience, usually an older guy, who's pretty cynical and got dragged along by his wife, sitting there all night with his arms folded to show he's not too happy about being there. But then the miracle happens: 'I've got your dad here, says his name's Brian. He's telling me he was a bit of a gambler and boozer and used to give you a bit of grief when you were younger.'

By this stage the man in the audience will be sitting up, his arms not so tightly folded any more. I carry on bringing forth more details, and then comes the clincher: 'You never got his approval but he wants me to tell you, "Well, just tell him I'm proud of him. I wish I'd said it while I was here. And I love him to pieces."'

At that point, the man in the audience bursts into uncontrollable tears and can't stop shaking, because he's finally heard what he's always wanted to hear. We have proved that his dad's in spirit, because of all the little details we've been told by spirit; and everyone in the audience can sense the chemistry between the man and the person in spirit. For me, that is really, really cool. To heal hearts: that's my purpose, that's what spirit does.

I think you only ever want to be, or you only ever want to feel, wanted in life. You need to feel as if you're here for a reason. This kind of story has personal resonance for me, as the day my own dad came along to one of my shows was one of the biggest days of my life. I'd never felt approved of until then. But Dad loved the show, told me he was proud of me, and now he's even got a little corner of his house that's full of photos, articles about me, and my books. I can't tell you how much that means to me.

The fundamental quality

I also believe love is the fundamental spiritual quality. When I'm connecting with spirit, it's pure love that I encounter. I feel so lucky to have that experience. It's like knowing God – it *is* knowing God – when you feel that kind of love.

What is love? It is the great unifying force. It's the quality that makes us not alone in the universe. And when we connect with spirit, we know in the deepest way we possibly can that all things are connected, and that we are connected to all things.

I ride motorbikes. Sometimes I like to hop on my bike, with my son on the back, and head off for a whole day. It's a meditation for me because in that moment I have no issues, there is nothing happening for me outside that experience. I feel the wind on my face, I smell the freshness of the countryside, I have my favourite songs running through my head. I am at one with the machine; I am totally in the zone. I feel at one with the world.

There is one simple goal above everything else in spiritual awareness, and for us humans it's the hardest one of all: to love unconditionally. We love our children, our families, our friends – but what about the rest of the planet? To love unconditionally means to love without conditions: that is, no judgement, no ifs, buts or maybes.

In the Lord's Prayer we ask to be delivered from evil, and I truly believe that what this means is that we're asking God to deliver us from our own judgementalism and our negativity towards others who perhaps don't live up to our expectations. Much evil is done in the world through the negative judgements of one person or group over another. We can ask God, or spirit, to help free us from that negativity and to cultivate an attitude of acceptance and forgiveness – in a word, love.

Non-judgement, forgiveness and love – these are the ultimate goals, and the ultimate challenges. We all know the limitations of being human! We easily get caught up in conflicts, we get angry over our losses. We say things like, 'Why me?' and 'I can't take this any more!' Ever been to that stage in your life where it's just too much?

But you're a survivor. You're still here. The Bible tells us, if you seek you will find. Set your spiritual goals, and then ask for help. That's what praying is. That's what meditation is. That sounds like an action plan to me! And remember, the process is the message: set aside your expectations; go with the flow. If you go looking for love in your own heart you will surely find it; when you make time to connect with spirit, you will find unconditional love.

The unbreakable bond

Does it seem strange to you that a person in spirit should go on being concerned about the well-being of his family? When you think about it, it's the most natural thing in the world. The bond between the person in spirit and the people left behind is purely built out of love. If there is no love, there is no connection. And I have found that, given the love connection, spirit are very concerned with their loved ones and want them to be happy and to live good lives.

An example of this came during a reading when a man came through to communicate with his wife and adult daughter. He was a lovely man, very easy to talk to, and he told me many details of his earthly life that left his wife and daughter in no doubt that it really was him that I was speaking to.

As a boy, this man came from a very unhappy family. In fact, he'd left home at 15, got on a boat and came to New Zealand all by himself. He had a good life here, working as a bus driver. As you can imagine, his feeling for the family that he built here was especially strong. He recalled doing jigsaws with his daughter, and told her, through me, that he was with her now whenever she sat down to do a puzzle. He remembered his happy marriage, and acknowledged how hard they'd worked at their relationship. He acknowledged how his upbringing had affected him, making him reclusive at times, and a bit emotionally shut down.

Yet it was clear there had been real romance in their lives. His wife had been engaged to someone else when he came along, but when she met him he made her feel better about herself, so she dropped her first fiancé and married this man. 'I still want you,' he told her, through me.

His message to his family was that he wanted them to organise a reunion: 'Have a good celebration of our lives. Don't drift apart, make the effort.' Even in spirit, his belief in a strong family was still powerful.

The most moving part, though, was when he told his daughter how proud he was of her and how he wished he'd been around to meet her son. However, I was getting a powerful feeling of a girl child as well, and asked, 'Where is the little girl?'

It turned out that she had lost a baby girl, and that her daughter was now with her father in spirit. Her father cradled his arms to show how he was looking after her.

Love in a pink cardie

KAY

Missing Bruce, her husband of 39 years, Kay did everything she could to try and make a connection with him, and with her mother. She came along to one of my shows carrying several items that had belonged to her mother, as well as some meaningful mementos of her husband: a fob watch she had given him, a one pound note she found in a treasure box in his drawer, and a threepence her mother had given her for luck on her wedding day, which she'd also found in her husband's box. But the most obvious thing – and the thing that first caught my eye – was her bright pink cardie. What I didn't know was that it had been knitted by Bruce himself. He was, Kay told me, 'a fabulous knitter' and the cardie was the last thing he knitted, during his 10 years of illness.

I don't know if it was because of Kay's forethought, but Bruce certainly came through for her. First her mother came, but she immediately brought Bruce. Bruce, Kay told me later, was tall, handsome – and very shy. She didn't really need to tell me he was shy – instead of coming right up to me and standing by me on stage, Bruce hid behind my whiteboard. 'I'm not coming out there,' he told me. All I could see were his legs in spirit.

This is not uncommon – spirits manifest as they were in life so that we can be sure it's them. How many of us, living, would want to get on stage in front of hundreds of people? It's no wonder our spirit loved ones often prefer to hide behind curtains, or pillars, or whiteboards. In fact, when I told the audience that Bruce was hiding, Kay nudged her son and daughter-in-law and said, 'That would be him to a tee.'

But eventually Bruce relaxed and we began to have a really lovely reading. He came because of his love for his family. He was someone who had clung to life as long as he could, and he said, first up, that he was angry that his medical treatment hadn't been different. Later Kay told me that this was quite right – there had been difficulties and she'd had real concerns that he wasn't getting the treatment he needed. He'd wasted away to a shadow of his former self. 'But,' Bruce told me, 'I've got it all back now. I'm good as gold now.'

He showed us several things that proved to his family it was indeed him. I got an impression of polishing cars, and his son told us that he had had a 1952 Chevy that he'd owned for 45 years. 'It was his pride and joy.' An image I got of a garage was probably Bruce's father's garage, where father and son were 'always under a car together'.

But at a certain point in the reading, things became less clear and Kay was mystified by a couple of the messages that came through. 'No,' she said, when Bruce mentioned a name, Jo. 'Jo? No.' She was sure there were no Jos in their family. And then, when Bruce mentioned the name 'Margaret' in connection with his own mother, Kay again was sure there were no significant people of that name.

This is where faith comes in. It's difficult sometimes to be up on stage and be told 'no' to messages, especially if it's an image or a name that is coming through very insistently from spirit. Often, spirit shouts a name at me, yet the person in the audience shakes their head in confusion. Years of experience have taught me not to worry – these things usually get sorted out eventually, and I often get emails and letters from people who have finally realised what spirit was talking about.

That's what happened here. Kay went home and rang her aunt to tell her about the reading. Her aunt reminded her that their mother's father had died when their mother was very young and she had a feeling he might have been Jo. She called back later to say, no, their grandfather's name had been Ernest ... but he was always known by his nickname Jo!

That was a real possibility, as Bruce had been brought through by Kay's mother and they had always been very close. And then another possibility appeared. When Kay rang Bruce's sister Moya to tell her about the reading, she said, 'Bruce used to call me Jo!' – and Kay remembered that was true. So:

suddenly there were two very close Jos to choose from.

The 'Margaret' connection was quite funny. It turned out that Bruce's mother had been very keen on Bruce marrying a woman called Margaret. In fact, even when Bruce and Kay were on their honeymoon, she rang Kay's mother to say that Margaret should have been her son's choice. It seems that Bruce's mother is still holding the candle for Margaret! Somehow I don't think her matchmaking will go any better in the spirit realm than it did here on earth, judging by the huge love I felt coming from Bruce for his family.

Kay had nursed her husband for 10 years, watching the once physically strong man – who had played cricket for Auckland – succumb to Parkinsons-like symptoms and dementia. She was absolutely thrilled to have this communication from him. 'I feel really happy and settled,' she says. 'I know he's with me. I quite often feel he's with me. I feel protected.'

They knew you were there

It's not always possible for someone to say goodbye to their loved ones before they pass. In fact, the most common messages that spirit bring to me during my readings is that they didn't get the chance to say goodbye, and that they want to communicate the love and appreciation they have for the people they left behind. This message is such a common part of readings, but I never lose my appreciation for its power. It's a miracle, is it not? It can change lives, and it can heal those left behind.

There are various reasons why someone who is passing might not get the chance to say goodbye to their loved ones. It might be a matter of physical distance, or it might be that they were involved in an accident and the death was sudden, or perhaps illness robbed them of the power to communicate.

What I can tell you is this: if you have sat at the side of someone who is dying, and held their hand and talked to them and stroked their face, even if that person is unconscious, they still knew you were there. Time and time again I have passed on messages from spirit who want to thank their loved ones for the love they showed at their bedside. I have so often received the sensation of the stroking of face or hair or hand, and the living person has agreed that they were doing that to the dying person. I look at it this way: when you love a baby, the baby can't speak to you, but no one has any doubt that the baby feels loved, feels secure, warm, happy – all the good things that come with being loved. It's the same when someone is dying. They may have lost the power of speech, they may be lying there with their eyes closed, but they will feel the love you have for them. I know they do, because time and time again, they tell me, and they show their appreciation for the person who looked after them in that vulnerable state.

They know what's going on for us

The spirits of our loved ones continue to watch over us.

There were two women sitting together in the audience one night, a mother and her daughter, and the mother was holding a framed photo of her own mother. I sensed that there were some strong spirits present around these two. I got an image of the Eiffel Tower, which to me symbolises France, and at the same time I saw images of military medals. The spirit presence was male, and so I guessed he had served in the Second World War. He told me he had been dead a long time and had missed out on many things, especially meeting his grandchildren.

The older woman in the audience agreed this was her father. His message to her was, 'Thank you for looking after your mother.' It turned out that her mother had been ill for a while before dying on the operating table, and so hadn't had the chance to say goodbye.

The mother came through, too, and I could tell she had been an amazing woman, very caring and lots of fun. In fact, I was getting a sensation of 'sister', and the woman in the audience agreed that they'd been more like sisters than mother and daughter. Her mum told her, 'I'm safe with your dad now, and I'm very happy because I had missed him so much, all those years when he'd gone ahead of me. I want to say thank you for looking after me when I was sick, and I will always love you and be with you.'

Then the woman in spirit turned her attention to her granddaughter, the younger woman in the audience. The woman in spirit was giving me the feeling that her granddaughter had two children, and she was laughing. I asked the young woman if it was correct that she had two children, although I felt a bit uncertain because her grandmother was laughing so much.

'Only one,' the granddaughter said. 'But I'm pregnant at the moment! It was a secret. Thanks Gran!' But she seemed happy to have her secret blown in this way.

'It's her way of saying she's watching over you,' I told her.

The proof is in the reading

Our people in spirit love us. There is no doubt about this, and I see the proof in every reading I do. The effort that it takes spirit to meet us in the zone between the worlds is proof in itself – they come with love, and they come with effort, and they come with messages that show they are watching us live our daily lives, and want us to be happy.

I was doing a show in Hamilton, and there was a man sitting in the middle of the audience who seemed to have many spirits around him. He was a real salt-of-the-earth character, a really down-to-earth guy, and to tell the truth, I knew he was feeling a bit uncomfortable, if not downright sceptical, about being where he was. His dad was there in spirit for him, though, and then his mum also came through, and then his younger brother. As I mentioned his younger brother, he kind of sat up and really started to pay attention.

'There's a connection here with boxing,' I said. 'Was your brother a boxer?'

'Yes,' the man agreed, suddenly looking a bit teary. 'He loved boxing, and we used to go to the gym together.' For him, that was the evidence that proved the connection was real. Now that he was more sure of what was going on, it was time for spirit to give him the message they had come for.

'Your mum has come through with an image of fishing,' I told him. I focused for a minute. 'I don't think she means that you actually go fishing, but it's more an indication that you need to take time out – that you need some downtime. You're not taking enough time for yourself.'

The man looked not only a bit shocked, but was quite emotional and it was clear that this message had hit the nail on the head.

'Also,' I went on, 'she's now talking about patience. She's telling me that this is one of the hardest things in your life, as it is for many of us.'

The man nodded, and I knew that this message was as real to him as if his mother was physically standing right in front of him, such is the power of genuine spiritual connection.

'Your mum is telling you to have more patience, to be kinder not only to those around you, who are often doing their best, but also to be kinder to yourself. Don't be so hard on yourself. Be more accepting of yourself and others, and focus more on what you've got, rather than on what you haven't achieved yet.'

This was a powerful message. For me, messages like this from spirit are absolute proof of their love and concern for us. We never need to feel unloved, or even alone. When we remember our loved ones, they are there for us, watching over us, and they want only the best for us.

So much to be grateful for

Communicating with spirit through prayer and meditation is a wonderful gift – but how often do we forget to express our thanks for that gift? Or, indeed, how often do we forget to even feel gratitude for the many wonderful things in our life?

EXERCISE

In your notebook, take a clean page and write down all the things in your life that you are grateful for. No ifs or buts. Don't let your grumpy little voice sneak in and undermine you. Sure, we've all got things in our lives that are not perfect, or even good

– but this is not the place to be giving them any space. This page is for the good things.

Look around you, at your home, your children, your family, your friends, your garden, the park down the road, your favourite coffee bar, your favourite thing to eat, the best song in the world, the singing of birds, a beautiful dress that's hanging in your wardrobe, a gorgeous motorbike that's parked in your garage. Don't hold back! Nothing can be too big or too little to put on this page.

When you've finished, close your eyes, take some of those deep, meditative breaths that you're getting so good at, and really feel your way into the truth of what you've written. Allow yourself to feel the joy that these things bring you; and then allow yourself to feel gratitude to spirit, God, the universe, life itself, for giving you these good things.

It's so important to be thankful. And the wonderful truth of it is, if you focus on the things in your life that you're grateful for, you get a certain kind of feeling – of happiness, euphoria, even. It's a wonderful sensation. You're tuned in, your frequency is up. It is a very spiritual feeling. It is a very peaceful place to be.

Gratitude is something we can take easily into our everyday lives. Walking prayers are the perfect expression of it – the little prayers you say on the fly. For instance, I look at my house – and, remember, I used to be homeless – and I am so thankful. So I say it out loud: 'Thank you!'

When something goes well for you – a social get-together, a business meeting, a harmonious exchange with your teenager – just say a quick 'thank you'. It is right to be thankful, and it also reminds us of the good in our life. Make gratitude a habit – you'll enjoy your life more, and you will feel the presence of spirit in your life. The act of practising gratitude raises our frequency level and literally puts us closer to spirit.

Let me share with you a funny thing I like to do in the mornings. Every morning I have a shower, and every morning of course the window in my bathroom steams up. So I take the opportunity to express my gratitude to spirit, and to build good feeling in my life. Using my finger, I just write 'Thanks, spirit'. I also draw a smiley face. Sometimes I put a big love heart and just say thanks. It's hard to do that when you're angry with the world, but if you religiously do it you start to release all that pressure and all the toxins inside of you; all the hurt, worry, pain, starts to go and you begin to accept. You feel a lot better. You're programming your mind to keep smiling.

My rule of thumb is that I'm grateful to spirit for what they provide for me. After all, without them I wouldn't be where I am.

In some cases I've written things like 'Help me to understand the anger that I'm feeling', 'Please guide me today' or 'Show me the way'.

The hardest one to write is, 'I love me', but writing it breathes some of those feelings into life and so it's good for me. The ultimate, after months of doing this religiously every day, is that I accept myself. I love me. I love spirit for showing me how to find myself.

Glass half full

The way we feel, the attitudes that we express in our daily life, and the love that we bring to our encounters, all have a tangible effect on the world around us. Love for ourselves becomes a loving attitude that incorporates everything. Love is the great unifier, and spirit is the purest form of love.

Years and years ago I was offered a glass of water by an old priest. I drank half the glass and he asked me, 'How was that?' 'It was ... water,' I answered, slightly mystified.

He took another glass and filled it for himself, and then he said to me, 'Do what I do.' He put his hand over the glass and he said the Lord's Prayer. I did the same, and then I drank the water. The difference was unbelievable. The prayer – the act of asking for blessing, and of being thankful – had raised the vibrational tone of the water so that its effect on my body was quite different. When you give thanks for your food, it changes the dynamics. It was an incredible expression of the power of love and gratitude.

Meditation

FORGIVENESS – LOVE'S GREATEST ACTION

I ask that my heart be freed of negative and painful emotions. I ask for the generosity to let go of all resentment, and I ask for the strength to truly forgive those who have hurt me. I ask for help in forgiving myself of the things I feel ashamed of, and I ask for guidance in creating a more positive energy for myself and for the world.

Have you ever had the experience of facing someone who's hurt you and telling them from your heart that you forgive them?

Is there someone in your life that you need to forgive? Someone who has wronged you – and, more importantly, someone whose wrong actions you carry around in your heart like a little shot of poison? Take this situation with you into your meditation.

Do your foundational work so that you feel safe and calm and protected. When you are ready, acknowledge how much this person has hurt you. Imagine how good it would be to be free of this hurt. Experience the hurt they have caused you, and then breathe out slowly while imagining yourself letting go of this hurt. Breathe it out.

Feel yourself actually start to loosen inside as that poison is expelled from your body.

You know fully that this hurt you are carrying, while triggered by the actions or inactions of this person, is actually a creation of your own imagination. You and only you have breathed life into this hurt. You can release it. You are the power within your own life.

Imagine yourself calmly telling this person that they have hurt you and that you have carried around this hurt, but now you are releasing it. Imagine yourself telling them that you forgive them. Feel the truth that this act of forgiveness is an enormous benefit to yourself – you are freeing yourself of the poison of resentment and anger. You have moved closer to spirit, you have replaced anger with unconditional love.

You will feel the benefit of this meditation immediately. However, in my experience, feelings that you've carried around for a long time can take a lot of work to truly dislodge. Don't worry if those feelings come sneaking back – forgiveness is one of the hardest things to practise. But if they come back, don't be afraid of them. Acknowledge them – say, 'Oh, there you are again.' You know what to do, and you know that if you keep practising this meditation the feelings in it will become a habit and will replace those other uncomfortable feelings. Your new habit of thinking and feeling will lead to freedom.

When you feel truly free of those negative feelings, and truly forgiving, you might like to talk to this person and tell them you forgive them. But make sure you have truly found forgiveness in your heart before you attempt a face-to-face encounter! Any residual bitterness will be carried to the meeting in the form of expectation, and you might not get the response that you want.

I would never want to belittle the spiritual effort it takes to forgive. But if you can find forgiveness in your heart, you have found one of the most powerful expressions of love that there is.

STEP TEN

Follow the path

Life is not having and getting, but being and becoming.

–Matthew Arnold, English poet

'Kelvin,' came a very insistent voice from the auditorium. I looked up and saw a sprightly elderly woman sitting a few rows back, waving her hand in the air. 'Kelvin, I'm 84, and I want to know if there's anyone there for me?'

As she spoke, I was instantly swept by an overwhelming sensation of love. 'You've lost your husband,' I said to her. 'He is waiting for you.'

The feelings I was getting from her husband in spirit were especially strong, and into my head came an image of something I'd seen earlier that day: a pair of beautiful white doves. They belong to a friend of mine, and she'd named them Mr and Mrs Lovey Dovey – go figure! When I saw them, I was struck by the bond between them – a bond that seemed to symbolise what I was feeling from this woman's husband. So I went to my whiteboard and wrote 'Mr and Mrs' on one line, and 'Lovey Dovey' below. There was a space next to 'Mr and Mrs'.

'What does Jack mean to you?' I asked the woman.

'That's our surname!' she said. So I wrote 'Jack' next to 'Mr and Mrs' in the space I'd left. I love this kind of happening – it is my proof that spirit has planned everything, and I am just the conduit.

Mr and Mrs Jack – Norma and Trevor – had been married for 64 years. Talking to her, it was clear that she had nothing but happy memories and admiration for the man she'd lived with for so long. He was an extremely bright, intelligent man who had left his body to the Medical School as a 'give back', so that he could continue to serve a purpose even after death.

He was, Norma told me, the kind of man who could fix anything. He was an inventor, a lateral and creative thinker with an intensely inquiring mind who made friends wherever he went. He also had a special gift: he could 'talk' to birds and dogs. He'd whistle to birds in aviaries and they'd all come flocking down to him – aviarists and zookeepers told him they'd never seen anything like it. I believe some people are gifted in this way – my own father is gifted with dogs, and even savage dogs are calm towards him.

From talking to Trevor in spirit, I believe he was an advanced soul – I could feel his wisdom and kindness and great love.

His daughter Helen, who was with Norma at the show that night, told me her father had been a non-believer in spirit during his lifetime, although his mother had visited clairvoyants. However, on his deathbed, it seems his inquiring mind got the better of him.

He said to Helen, who was lying beside him, 'I wonder how this is going to work out? Dying and everything? What will happen? I wonder if I'll just be dead, or if anything happens.'

Helen said, 'I told him what I'd heard others say: "From what I've learned about it, someone that loves you very much will come and get you. The light comes, a big moonbeam comes down and you just jump into the light. When you get there, will you let us know?"

'A short time later, when he was on the point of dying – really on his last breath – he suddenly said, "Mum! Mum!" It was said in the way you'd say, "Mum's here!" Like it was a surprise. And I said to him, "Step into the light. It's time to fly."'

During the reading, Trevor told me he watches over Norma at night while she's sleeping, and this fitted perfectly with Norma's experience since her husband had died.

When he first died, he came and lay beside her in bed at night, a comforting presence. Since then, he comes often and stands at the foot of her bed. Now he appears as a being all in white, and she can no longer see his face, but she feels that it is him. Helen says, 'Maybe he's getting his angel wings!'

One of the things Trevor wanted me to pass on to his wife was, 'We should not be afraid of the afterlife.' So, just as Helen had asked, he did come back to let her know.

Norma didn't know what to expect from the show, apart from hoping that she might hear something from Trevor. She was amazed at what happened. Trevor asked me to give her a message. 'He says to tell you, "I loved you as soon as I saw you, and I love you now as much as I ever did",' I told her, and she gasped. 'That was exactly what he wrote to me. I've got that written down and tucked into a book at home.'

As the reading was ending, Trevor popped one final image into my mind. I was a bit mystified, but I have to trust spirit, even when what they tell me seems odd at best.

'Okay,' I said, 'now I have to ask you something very unusual. Trevor is holding out his hand and on it is an apple cucumber...'

Well, I didn't need to worry. Norma and Helen both gasped in surprise and recognition. Trevor was a very keen gardener, and apple cucumbers were his speciality. He had a special variety and saved seeds for his daughter. His family had been market gardeners, and Trevor had been seriously interested in gardening, with a passion for grafting.

'He loved his gardening,' Helen told me. 'I felt the cucumbers were a symbol of that, or reminding me to get going and plant some of his seeds.'

Trevor's message of love for his wife and daughter was a reminder that love continues even after the body's death, and that love is, indeed, the connection between this world and the next. It reminds me that we must cherish every moment of time we have with the ones we love so that we can live without regret. It doesn't mean we won't miss them when they pass on – Norma continues to sorely miss Trevor – but it helps to know that the love we had here on earth continues in spirit.

A pause between drinks

I asked spirit to help me understand the world. Spirit showed me a beautiful white light, and a pathway, and so I took it. It took me to a place where I felt only unconditional love: no judgement, no negativity; only safety and compassion. In that place I met my own ancestors and I believe I met Jesus Christ himself. I saw that, after we pass, we cross into that new realm of healing and forgiveness.

When we pass out of this life, it's not an end. When we say goodbye to our loved ones, it's not an end. It's like a pause between drinks; or an intermission at the movies.

Passing is just a transition, from the physical to the spiritual plane. Our soul leaves our earthly physical body behind and carries on into the white light – just as a caterpillar in a chrysalis transforms into a butterfly.

We don't know when this change will take place. I believe that before we were born into our physical bodies we sat with the Creator and mapped out our life here on earth. We chose the challenges, the things from which we need to learn – but as soon as we were born, we forgot.

So, as we move through life, we need to learn to accept the things that happen to us, to grow from our challenges, and to trust that everything is part of the plan that we ourselves have laid out.

Our lives, with all their busy-ness and their material concerns, take us away from spirit. We forget that we are here for God's purpose: to love, to forgive, to grow, to reach our full potential as human beings so that eventually we, too, can achieve our angel wings and cease the cycle of reincarnation.

The wheel of life

I did not begin when I was born, nor when I was conceived. I have been growing, developing, through incalculable myriads of millenniums. All my previous selves have their voices, echoes, promptings in me.

–Jack London, author and social activist

Can I prove reincarnation? No. But I believe in it. I know that our souls live on after death – I speak to the spirits of those who have passed, and I have been shown where they go to be healed until they are ready to return to an earthly form. But these things can be difficult for us to understand.

What say someone passes, and is then reincarnated within a generation or two? Will the family of that person who has passed still be able to communicate with that spirit if it has already reincarnated? Who are we actually speaking to?

My answer to that, and it comes not from me but from spirit, is that since we are all created by the Creator and we are the children of the Creator, the Creator does not leave us without hope. Therefore, because the Creator is almighty, he or she (and such gender terminology is irrelevant) takes a blueprint of each one of his or her children so that when you come to see somebody like me, regardless of whether Dad's reincarnated or not, you will be able to talk to him.

In other words, the Creator will be showing me your dad like a hologram. If there's a blueprint then you're not left without that love, you're not left without hope and you're certainly not left alone. That love is still unconditional.

As I say, we can't prove reincarnation, but your soul already knows the answer. When you meet someone and you just instantly want to hug and embrace them, it's because you've had a wonderful experience together before.

I have seen my past lives through my third eye – and this is something you will be able to do, too. When we accept that we have had a past life but that we've chosen to come back to gain more knowledge, our lives automatically become more meaningful. We embrace life and we're thankful for it. The past is the past, sure enough; but we know we need to learn from it.

Could tomorrow be the day you've chosen for your earthly life to end? That's a really big thing to think about. What say you have chosen tomorrow? Will you be happy with the way you've lived this life, with what you have become, or will you be one of the people who say, 'I wish I'd done more with my life?'

Many of us live blindly, as if we think life goes on forever, and as if our chances to do the things we want, to have the relationships we want, are endless and limitless. Well, they are limitless, but they are not endless. And this is where I think that if we can accept that we will pass, and that we don't know when we have chosen for that passing, it will help us live more fully. I don't want to be one of the people who, on their deathbed, are filled with regret for the chances they never took; or who wish that instead of closing their minds, they had remained open to the limitless possibilities of the universe.

Scepticism

A woman in the audience was very surprised when her husband came through in spirit. She had come to the show hoping for a message from her mother, but her husband had been such a sceptic in life that she didn't for one minute expect to hear from him.

Well, guess what, would it surprise you to learn that human scepticism – in fact, any human ideology – doesn't survive the passage from this world to the next? Scepticism is just another human idea. Once we die and realise that our spirit lives on – which, by the way, is part of the Christian teaching about eternal life, is it not? – and that we still maintain a love connection with the people we've left behind, there is no place for scepticism. I've had many people come through who adhered to the Christian church's belief that spiritualism is somehow wrong or evil, but who, when they find themselves in spirit, realise that this is all part of God's wonderful plan for us. I've even had priests come through in spirit!

I don't really care if some people think what I do is wrong, or if they don't 'believe' in it. Their opinions don't alter my experience of communicating with spirit, through love, every day. I am happy talking to dead people. For me, they're not dead. They're certainly not monsters. They have the same souls they had when they were living here among us on earth – so how can it be bad to talk to them? It's only bad when your own intention is bad, or if you fail to put adequate protection around yourself and others. But if your intention is to understand, to help heal, it can only be good. It's all about love.

As for religion, I don't think it matters what religion you believe in as long as you're doing good in the world. Religion is an expression of the people practising it and may or may not have much to do with the loving spirit or God or the Creator who lies at the heart of things. Rule number 1: we're all going to the same place!

Anyway, back to my story. The woman was surprised but very happy when her husband came through. 'He didn't think of this stuff before he passed,' she said. 'He was in fear of where he was headed.'

The man talked about how he loved his wife and how much he missed their life together – they had been a private couple, just the two of them at home together. One thing was bothering me during this communication, and that was a little budgie that kept flying around me in spirit. I decided I had to ask the woman if there was any connection between her husband and a budgie. She was even more surprised and said that yes, they had a budgie but it got caught on one of those sticky papers you put out for flies. 'It had very few feathers left. He felt terrible about that!' she said, as the audience roared with laughter.

This story reminded me of another funny thing that happened during a show in Australia. I was doing a reading for a woman whose mother and father had both come through, and then I also felt the strong presence of a bird – this time, a cockatoo. And at that exact moment, I began to feel very, very cold. I told the woman what was happening, and asked her why she thought I was experiencing such an intense feeling of cold.

She gasped, 'Oh my God, the cockatoo! I left it in the freezer!' It turned out that when her bird had died very soon after her parents, she had been unable to part with it, so she wrapped it up and put it in the freezer. And there it stayed.

I believe we have a plan, a mission, for this life. It's what we worked out with the Creator before we came here in this physical form; it's what we must spend this earthly life discovering.

Eleanor Roosevelt said, 'You must do the thing you think you cannot do.' She said, 'You gain strength, courage and confidence by every experience in which you really stop to look fear in the face.'

Making time in your daily life for spirit is part of awakening yourself to the wonders of life, the truth about the universe and your own place in it, and to your own potential. I hope that this book has given you a key to begin the process of connecting with spirit. I can't stress enough that nothing worth this much will happen overnight. It takes discipline – the discipline to practise, and to keep going with faith and trust – and it takes self-knowledge. Eventually it will bring you a more satisfying, richer life both here in the day to day, and in terms of your spirituality. You will feel your connectedness to the universe and to your loved ones who have gone before you.

Only you can make the decision to set out on this path. But if you do, spirit will support you. Think of them, and they're there. Please don't shut them out, or belittle them by thinking that they're not there. Ask to be open, ask to be clothed in a robe of white light. Make time for spirit and be consistent with your practice. You won't fail.

Meditation

NOTICING AND CONNECTING

I ask for the blessing of the angels of the white light to guide and protect me. I ask for my tupuna, my ancestors, to look after me.

I ask for friends and family in the spirit world to show me what I need to learn today and help me to get closer to them, and to the understanding of spiritualism, and to show me how to empower myself.

I ask to be still in mind, to be balanced, to be protected from all that doesn't serve me. I ask for support when I make the decision to push my own self-imposed boundaries. I ask for courage.

Meditating is awesome, and there's no doubt you can travel anywhere in your own mind. You can visualise and experience anything you like. Sitting in your room, you can meet spirit and have the most amazing conversations with your loved ones who have passed. Spirit can tell you about the past, the future, and help you to live life in the best way possible.

But there is something really incredible about actually putting yourself out into the world, opening your mind and your heart to the environment around you and the feelings associated with it. We can all forget, or become oblivious to, the amazing things that go on around us. Putting ourselves out into the world can help us become more sensitive and more attuned to ourselves and to spirit.

I've written elsewhere in this book about the spiritual experience I enjoy on my motorbike. If you're in a car, you look at the countryside and you go, 'Oh, what lovely green grass' – but on a motorbike you can *smell* the grass, smell the cows and the smoke that's wafting across the paddocks. You actually become a part of it.

So, one of my favourite things ever is to meditate at the beach. All my senses are on fire – I'm smelling the salt and even tasting it on my lips; my toes love the feeling of the sand, I can hear the waves crashing and the seagulls calling – and I can feel the wind. I feel that I have totally become a part of my surroundings.

It's time to try it! Go to your favourite beach. If it's summer and the beach is likely to be crowded, take yourself there really early in the morning. Take a blanket so you won't get cold. Draw a circle in the sand with your foot and sit inside the circle. This is highly protective. You will feel extremely safe.

Say your prayer, and begin your meditation in the usual way. I consider this to be a noticing and connecting meditation. As you breathe, become super aware of all those things I've just mentioned: the sound of the waves, the feel of the breeze, the seagulls calling to each other.

The waves in particular play a big part in this meditation. Allow your mind to follow the sound of the waves, and take that sound right into your being. You are breathing slowly, in and out, and the waves are breaking and crashing inwards, and then drawing themselves back into the ocean. As you follow these sounds, your frequency lifts and your experience becomes increasingly intense.

Allow your thoughts to carry you upwards, through the clouds and into an appreciation of the space above you. You can ask, 'Is there anyone there for me?' Once you've asked, continue to do exactly as you've done before. You have no expectation. You are simply in this experience and you are waiting to see if anyone will come forward for you.

Give yourself permission to enjoy this moment, without calculating what you could be doing instead.

Sit in that beautiful place for as long as you want. When you have finished your meditation, thank spirit for sharing with you this sense of the oneness of yourself with the universe.

As you move into your daily life, and away from this meditation, you will feel that the high-frequency energy stays with you, and that you will have a heightened appreciation of your day. Your sense of connection to spirit will continue to sing within you, altering your personal vibration, attracting positive energy, and giving you the wonderful opportunity to positively affect the world.

We ask that the white light vortex be open over our lives, and that it keep us safe and give us strength and faith as we face our personal challenges. We give thanks to the spirits of our tupuna who have gone before us and who are always with us. We give thanks to our angelic realm for being there to protect us and look after us and share their knowledge with us. We give thanks for the opportunity to come closer to the unconditional love of spirit. Amen.

CONTACT DETAILS

Nigel Collis, clairvoyant and spiritual cleanser
Email: nigel@nigelcollis.co.nz
Phone: +64-9-831-0304 (Health World)
Mobile: +64-274-920-444
Postal address:
PO Box 84036
Westgate
Auckland
New Zealand

KELVIN
CRUICKSHANK
WALKING IN LIGHT

WALKING IN LIGHT

A powerful and compelling autobiography of Kelvin Cruickshank, psychic medium on the acclaimed TV2 series *Sensing Murder.*

As a child, Kelvin saw, heard and felt spirits, but had no idea what it all meant. He believed everybody could see and talk to ghosts.

Walking in Light shares Kelvin's memories of his earliest psychic experiences and his struggle to accept his gift. Years ago, after a complete breakdown, Kelvin finally acknowledged who he was and accepted his gift. With this, his life completely changed.

From his early days growing up in an isolated rural environment to travelling the world as an acclaimed psychic investigator, Kelvin's life story is amazing, inspirational and, at times, heart-breaking.

Kelvin gives an insight into the process of accessing the spirit world and answers some of the questions that he gets regularly asked at his events, shows and readings.

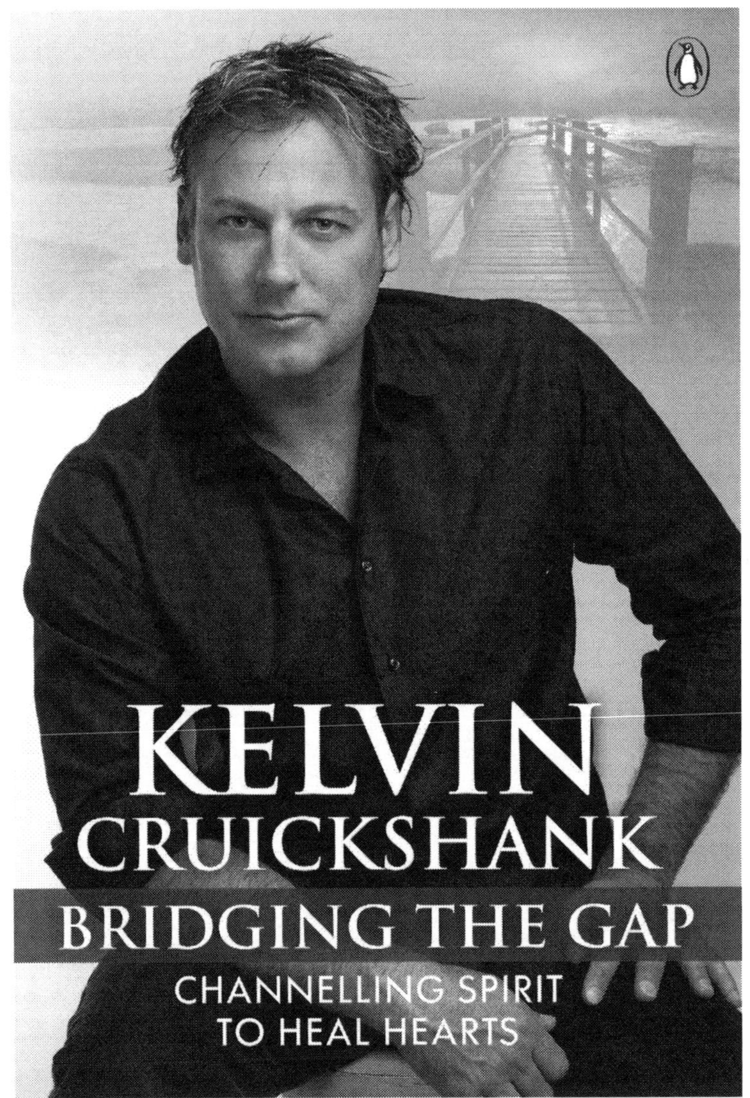

KELVIN
CRUICKSHANK
BRIDGING THE GAP
CHANNELLING SPIRIT
TO HEAL HEARTS

BRIDGING THE GAP

'It is very important to me to enable people to understand that there is nothing to fear in death. Life and love are eternal, and there is another world waiting for us when we pass on from this earthly existence.'

Kelvin Cruickshank, psychic medium on the acclaimed TV2 series *Sensing Murder,* and author of the bestselling *Walking in Light,* recounts incredible stories about helping people who are struggling to move on from the death of a loved one. The results have been amazing – people have had their lives changed and hearts healed by the contact. Some of the stories are heartbreaking, some are uplifting, but all are inspiring.

Books For ALL Kinds of Readers

At ReadHowYouWant we understand that one size does not fit all types of readers. Our innovative, patent pending technology allows us to design new formats to make reading easier and more enjoyable for you. This helps improve your speed of reading and your comprehension. Our EasyRead printed books have been optimized to improve word recognition, ease eye tracking by adjusting word and line spacing as well as minimizing hyphenation. Our EasyRead SuperLarge editions have been developed to make reading easier and more accessible for vision-impaired readers. We offer Braille and DAISY formats of our books and all popular E-Book formats.

We are continually introducing new formats based upon research and reader preferences. Visit our web-site to see all of our formats and learn how you can Personalize our books for yourself or as gifts. Sign up to Become A RHYW Registered Reader.

www.readhowyouwant.com

18771433R00142

Printed in Great Britain
by Amazon